# A Guide for People on the Autism Spectrum & Their Allies

# FINDING YOUR SUPERPOWERS

## ANNE PFLUG

# FINDING YOUR SUPERPOWERS

## A Guide for People on the Autism Spectrum & Their Allies

All marketing and publishing rights guaranteed to and reserved by:

**FUTURE HORIZONS**

(817) 277-0727

(817) 277-2270 (fax)

E-mail: info@fhautism.com

www.fhautism.com

ISBN: 9781957984339

# ACKNOWLEDGMENTS

This book would not have been possible without the presence in the world and contributions of my grandson, Trent; the COVID Pandemic; the work of Julia Cameron; Carla Thomas; Derek Lutz; those who agreed to review the early drafts and be interviewed; and my creative partners—Rand, Nancy, and Sandy. We would not have made it this far without the lifelong love and support of my family and second families.

I would also like to acknowledge the shared vision and contributions of Future Horizons, Inc. and Sensory World Publishing, as well as the affirming language and lived experience contributions of Freefall, Devin, Connor, and Rebecca, who encouraged the work and reviewed the content.

# TABLE OF CONTENTS

## CHAPTER 3: FINDING YOUR SUPERPOWERS
### page 53

## CHAPTER 4: PUTTING IT ALL TOGETHER
### page 77

●●●

# CHAPTER 1

# INTRODUCTION

# WHY THIS GUIDE?

I started this book when my grandson, who has lived with me virtually all his life and is autistic, was twenty-one years old. I have reflected on and continue to reflect on our journey together and what we have learned along the way. I realized that the most powerful positive "guiding light" for us has been my grandson's superpowers—auditory perfect pitch, mechanical/spatial reasoning, and hand-eye coordination. In addition to his ability to express himself in so many, mostly non-speaking ways. Somehow he always "knew" (and showed me) what was best for him at each stage in his life. My job was to figure out what he "knew" and nurture that knowledge in our everyday lives.

I want other families to be able to build on what we have learned. The spectrum and its impact on our lives has very real and difficult challenges. Making it a little easier for others seems a kindness. If there is anything I have learned from 2020 and life with COVID, it is that kindness matters.

I wanted my child to have as much resilience and independence as possible as an adult. That meant we needed to spend time throughout their life building a way of living that works for **them** (not necessarily for the typical world or my world). We needed to fight for it. I needed to learn how to affirm and encourage stimming and focused interests. It meant that my child needed to find their place in "Autistic culture" and with those who share his interests—their tribe. It meant we needed to explore a wide range of experiences and environments, beyond those I was comfortable with, so that they could discover what gives them joy, satisfaction, and peace. I needed to learn how to trust and support my child and their perception of the world—not discount or ignore them because their perceptions are different than mine. Now as an adult, I need to model taking care of myself, defining boundaries, and pursuing my interests so that they have an example to rely on when I am not there.

***(Reflections of a parent of a young autistic adult)***

# WHAT IS A SUPERPOWER?

**"SUPERPOWERS" AS REFERRED TO IN THIS BOOK ARE UNIQUE TO EACH INDIVIDUAL AND CERTAINLY NOT UNIVERSAL FOR ALL AUTISTIC PEOPLE.**

"Superpowers" as referred to in this book are unique to each individual and certainly not universal for all autistic people. Your unique superpowers come from your own character traits, focused interests, personal strengths, and abilities. **These "superpowers," like the original Superman, come from *your world*, not necessarily the neurotypical world here on earth.** They are yours to nurture and share as much, or as little, as you want. Some can emerge from the effects of autism on a person over their lifetime—effects on your brain, body, and senses like taste or vision. Others may come from inherited traits or those strengths that have emerged in your life so far. There may be more to come, as your life and interests change.

Many autistic differences create challenges that can make daily life overwhelming and difficult. The superpowers concept in this book is not intended to deny or discount the challenges that autistic people face every day—if anything, it is intended to affirm the strengths that an autistic person often develops to counter and/or address these very real and present challenges. Acknowledging and pursuing your abilities and strengths can provide positive energy, satisfaction, and wellbeing to balance some of the challenges of everyday life over the course of one's lifetime.

All human beings receive 11 million bits of sensory information every second of the waking day and have systems in their brain and body that manage and process that input.[1] In addition, every person has senses that are stronger or weaker. It is thought that people on the spectrum atypically have expanded and/or more suppressed senses that are different from the typical person's, accompanied by differences in brain, sensory, and thought processes. As a result, *autistic people often experience intense sensory input (or lack of input) from several or all of their senses, compared to the typical person. These intense sensory characteristics can be themselves "superpowers" or develop into "superpowers"* over a person's lifetime. Research on sensory and other strengths among autistic people is in its beginning stages. However, there are existing research findings related to positive character traits; the benefits that arise from pursuing focused interests; strengths in executive function, visual function, and auditory function; and a unique social intelligence system between autistic adults.[2] **Every autistic person is unique in their personal sensory experience, their personal traits, and the effects of autism they experience. The aim of this book is to help you and your allies discover and nurture your personal strengths—be they sensory abilities, personality traits or interests—to help you live a fuller and more satisfying life.**

For my grandson, his "hearing" or auditory sense system produces a sensitive and finely tuned auditory experience that includes perfect pitch. Perfect pitch occurs in one out of every 10,000 people but more often among those on the spectrum; his "visual" and 'touch' senses produce "super" eye-hand coordination. His detailed memory (trait or effect of ASD); and his spatial sense (vestibular) combined with the others produce, the capacity to "get"—as if by magic—mechanical processes, patterns and spatial relationships. He has pursued his strengths in a way that has led to self-confidence and direction in his life as an adult.

*Discovering and nurturing a person's superpowers can bring meaning to life, a feeling of positive self-worth and a "path" for a person to follow in contributing to their family and community life—the goal of this book.*

# SUPERPOWERS IN MODERN MEDIA

There has been an explosion in various forms of media and technology for and about people who are on the autism spectrum. I searched the word "autism" on Netflix and was overwhelmed by the number of television and movie entries. Some are better than others at portraying the spectrum experience. I especially love those that have actors or protagonists who are themselves autistic, like *As We See It*.[3]

*The Sniffer*[4] is one of my favorites. A less-affected autistic adult male uses his superpower of "smell" to provide odor-based clues for solving crimes. One of the episodes includes a child, about five or six, who is autistic and non-speaking. The child's repetitive behavior is used by a neurotypical relative to "commit" the crime. At the end of the episode, in a very sweet and sensitively portrayed sequence, one of the child's superpowers (spatial ability) is acknowledged and nurtured by the "Sniffer."

There are several shows that now star or have a primary male or female character who is an autistic person—young adults attempting transitions to independent living, a surgeon, a photographer, a detective, a chess champion, a lawyer, a software coder, an environmental advocate, etc.

*While many of the people portrayed in the media are on the part of the autism spectrum that is less affected by autism, every atypical person has one or more strengths, interests, and/or abilities that have gone unrecognized. Many can become their "superpowers." These positive traits are just waiting to be recognized, discovered, and developed.*

# RESOURCES

1. *Encyclopedia Britannica* "Human Physiology," retrieved from https://www.britannica.com/science/information-theory/Physiology.

2. See end of book for "References by topic" under "Strengths and Abilities."

3. *As We See It* Amazon Prime Video series 2022.

4. *The Sniffer* Netflix series 2013 to 2019

# CHAPTER 2

# SUPERPOWER TURNING POINTS

## ONE LIFE STAGE AT A TIME

In this chapter, we will explore human development at each stage of life or turning point. We will identify the developmental "job" of a person at each life stage and the issues that may arise for an autistic person. Every autistic person is unique, so for example, issues that may arise for one person at age five may appear for another at age ten or not at all. What appears in the text at each life stage are issues that have been identified most frequently either in the literature or in interviews conducted for this book.

At each life stage, a person affected by autism may need help to focus on and master the "job" of that particular developmental stage *and* address, if needed, issues that arise from the effects of autism. Help may come in the form of parents (or other allies, like teachers, therapists or specialized coaches) being aware of the child's learning "job" and finding ways to assist by providing experiences or methods that build developmental skill or knowledge. For example, early exposure to multiple social interactions with other children that are perceived by the autistic child as positive may increase the pleasure they get out of social interactions later in

life and lead to building a supportive group of friends as an adult. Note that girls and children of color are more often missed in early diagnosis, and parents and allies may need to be particularly diligent in seeking and confirming their child's diagnosis so that help is available to the child and family at as many life stages as possible. Several book interviewees noted that girls' autistic symptoms may be subtle in early years and in some cases masked by a child's ability to mimic neurotypical behavior.

At the same time, each developmental stage provides opportunities to identify "clues" about the individual's strengths or superpowers, either in the moment or retroactively. *As you read this part of the book, feel free to note clues you may have observed in yourself or through others' stories and memories. We will be using these "clues" as we go along to assemble a "picture" or "map" of your individual superpowers.*

Different flowers, plants, and trees thrive in the right combination of soil, water, and sunshine—in short, the right environment. Without the right environment plants do not reach their full potential, fail to thrive, or in the worst case, do not even germinate. People are the same way. The environment that gives one person what they need to thrive does not necessarily work for another person, leaving them to languish.  As caregivers, professionals, and educators—the adults in the room—our job is to find and create the right environment (soil, water, and sunshine) for each of the children in our care, so they can thrive.

In the case of autistic kids, creating a "thriving environment" can include first addressing pervasive pain, health and/or mental health conditions; lack of energy from sleep or food-related issues; sensory stressors and triggers; and then enabling self-regulation **prior to introducing** a learning task or activity. Sunshine is added by building trust, conveying respect, affirming differences, and communicating in the most effective way for the child's thinking style.

*(Observations of a seasoned educator)*

# BALANCING STIMMING, OR OTHER CALMING BEHAVIOR, AND USING YOUR SUPERPOWERS

*Experiencing atypical sensory input is often exhausting. It's exhausting for the autistic person and sometimes for those around them. That's why it's important to build stamina over time (and breaks for everyone) with calming behaviors.*

"Calming behavior," which includes "stimming," is a way for the body to organize itself, getting ready for tasks, or to join others. Calming behaviors are often repetitive actions that allow the mind (and body) to rest before taking on the "typical world". Calming behaviors can also sustain a person's use of their superpowers. To be effective, calming behaviors may need to occur in a different environment (room or special space) than your "typical world" activities.

Calming behaviors may use your superpowers as part of their coping mechanism. My grandson at twenty-one watches videos or plays video games that involve repetitive eye and/

or hand movement—his hand-eye coordination superpower. He especially likes repetitive spinning motion. Just writing this makes me a bit queasy, but for him, it's restful and refreshing. In his earlier years, he was fascinated by spinning objects and play equipment that spun his body around, and around, and around.

A person can have several or many calming behaviors. In early life stages, a child may use a set of calming behaviors that broaden or evolve over time. My grandson, when young, loved to make loud repetitive mono-syllable sounds (hearing sense), climb up high, flap his hands, rock his body, physically spin (visual), and be wrapped up tightly in a blanket (touch or proprioceptive senses). Some "stims" may appear to the "neurotypical" world (those without autism in this case) to be socially unacceptable and are often discouraged, especially in early life stages.[1] Interrupting or trying to suppress stimming and other calming behavior can lead to meltdowns or shutdowns. Being asked to "conform" to neurotypical behavior norms can also lead to anxiety, depression, and/or feelings of worthlessness.

Atypical adults may express their "calming" behaviors as stims; routines and rituals; insistence on sameness; focused interests; or simply solitary time to "chill". The type, amount of time, and frequency of "calming behavior" varies with each individual and sometimes with the level of anxiety in the moment. Over time, stamina can increase as you use your superpowers in the "typical world," expanding the length and/or intensity of time spent before resting through calming.

There are two sides to most autistic differences: a challenge in one context or environment may be a strength in another context or environment. You can experiment until you figure out how to use the strength and effective strategies to use when your strength becomes a challenge. Social messages that reinforce the idea that different or unconventional equals "wrong" are hard to shake. The human developmental life cycle naturally gives you several points in life to turn all or part of those social messages around and gain more of a positive sense of self as you learn about, use, master, and appreciate your personal strengths and abilities. Often autistic differences eventually reveal their strengths if you are patient, not just their challenges. *For example, a new mother who stims by rocking her body into adulthood found that her baby craved rocking, and they both got a high degree of satisfaction out of rocking together.*

**(Personal story of an adult with autism)**

For many autistic people, pent up stress, anxiety, depression, and frustration compounded by sensory overload or interruption of calming behavior can trigger a "meltdown" (external explosion) or "shutdown" (internal implosion). For autistic people, meltdowns can result in what is considered by the typical world to be heightened "outside the norm" physical or verbal behavior.[2] A shutdown is also an overwhelmed autistic person's response to their distress; however, the person gets quiet and less responsive as they block out extra stimuli. Shutdowns may proceed or follow meltdowns and are more often seen with girls, who can be more harshly punished for outwardly expressive behavior. Meltdowns and shutdowns can be dangerous, so it's important to learn the best reaction do's and don'ts.

Meltdowns and shutdowns are sometimes confused with tantrums, which are often short, require an audience, and end when the person gets what they want. Tantrums typically end after childhood. Tantrums may also occur when a person can-not express what they want with words. Meltdowns and shutdowns, on the other hand, are responses to distress and overload that may continue into adulthood.

In a "meltdown," the brain is controlled by its "flight or fight" mechanism. It narrows or rejects other methods of response that are more accessible by the same person in a calmer environment. For example, my grandson felt overwhelmed by conditions in his elementary school classroom one day and left the classroom (flight mechanism) to climb a 40-foot tree in the school yard, where he felt safe. My grandson had practiced climbing for years and was very good at it—especially for his age and size. The adults' reaction prolonged his meltdown, severely reducing his ability to respond to their requests to come down from the tree. He was not able to talk or move in this "flight" reaction state. It was not until talking and noise was significantly reduced, the number of people around the tree shrunk to one familiar person, and he was encouraged to stim for enough time to regain his ability to hear and talk that he was able to respond. A firefighter eventually climbed up the tree using a ladder and, without touching him (avoiding triggering a new and dangerous round of "flight"), helped my grandson to return to the ground. My grandson taught a lot of adults some significant things about autism that day. A week later, the school had a new personally selected and decorated cardboard appliance box that my grandson could "flee" to when overwhelmed with calming behavior materials inside. Over time, meltdowns decreased as more self-regulation strategies were acquired, and he was able to notice meltdown signals and act on them.

Apparently Neurotypicals are good at clumping a whole array of body movements, separate actions, and sensory expectations into something they consider to be one step. Autistics like me often break things down into lots of little steps. Each step comes with mental preparation for whatever sensory experience comes with that step. Unexpected unpleasant sensations are far more distressing than expected ones. Task breakup also incorporates the extra effort I need coordinating my body movements to not bang into or drop things. Funnily enough even though breaking everything down into these little steps sounds like it makes things harder and more exhausting, it makes things easier for me. The more my sensory issues are bothering me at that point in time, the smaller the steps need to be. Example (Making Coffee):

**Neuro-Typical:**
1. Make coffee
2. Drink coffee.

**Me:**
1. Turn on coffee maker. It will make soft humming and gurgling noises—expect them.
2. Check water tank level.
2a. Okay, it needs to be refilled.
2b. Slide it from the back of the coffee maker. Expect the feel of the hard plastic with both sharp and smooth corners, and the dragging sensation of moving it, and sounds that it makes.
2c. Carry it to the sink. The little bit of water left will slosh inside. That's a sensation I need to expect too.
2d. Take the lid off. It is hard and has sharp edges, so don't hold it wrong or too tight.
2e. Find an empty spot on the counter.
2f. Put the lid down in that empty spot. I may accidentally touch the counter. It will be hard and cold. The lid will make noise- plastic against countertop.
2g. Hold the tank under the faucet with one hand.
2h. Use your other hand to turn on the water. The faucet handle will be cold metal. The faucet will make a bad noise as the waster hisses out.
2i. The tank will get heavier as it fills, so adjust for that. Expect that I might accidently get cold water on my hand.
2j. Turn off the faucet.
2k. Use both hands on the tank.
2l. Find another empty spot on the counter.
2m. Put the tank down on the counter.
2n. Pick up the lid. Expect the feel and sound of it and the counter.
2o. Put the lid on the tank. The plastic will make clicking noises.
2p. Get a good grip on the tank.
2q. Pick the tank up carefully.
2r. Carry the tank to the coffee maker, keeping it level. It will slosh and may leak on my hands.
2s. Carefully, slot the tank under the cupboard and over the coffee maker.
2t. Lower the tank on the back of the coffee maker and slide it into the connector. It will make a soft sliding noise.

As you can see, I haven't even gotten the coffee going yet! I have many steps left to go.

I make coffee every single morning. It's one of the easier things for me to do. Having a Keurig makes a big difference in step reduction. However, if I am having especially severe sensory problems right from the morning get-go, I will forget steps and/or be extra uncoordinated. I have run the coffee maker without water in it, or worse, run it without a mug in it (big mess), and I have spilled water all over trying to get the water tank back on.

Now picture every single thing you do needing to be broken down like this, with some of those steps involving sensations you know are going to be unpleasant or even downright painful but that you are going to make yourself endure anyway. Know that there are things that the rest of the world thinks of as easy and will expect you to do, that you will just not be able to do. Know that if you overdo it, and have a public meltdown as an adult, the police may be called on you. Life is a lot harder with Autism.

*(Freefall, autistic young woman)*

# INCREASING STAMINA THOUGH SENSORY IMPACT MITIGATION

*The second life strategy you can come to rely on to limit the feeling of being overwhelmed by atypical sensory input is to incorporate habits and environmental changes into your home, community, and work lives that reduce or mitigate the intensity or lack of feeling experienced from your senses. Think of it as a "sensory budget"; if you limit your typical daily routine's sensory overload, then you have some of your "sensory budget" left for other activities (explore "Spoon Theory" for detailed examples related to pain). You may even be able to reduce the amount of time or frequency needed for calming behavior in your day, increasing stamina.*

In our household we have so many mitigation strategies now that it is hard for us sometimes to remember what is a part of the typical world and what is not.

Here are some examples:

## HEARING

Headphones or ear protection (ear plugs or muffs) to limit environmental and/or intense soaunds from such things as power equipment, screen-based audio, fire drills, or other people.

## TASTE

Food prepared in the same way with limited spice to reduce exposure to overwhelming taste or texture. Foods are not mixed or are presented with space between or in separate dishes. The same food may be served repetitively for the same meal every day or rotated slowly over time.

## VISION

Home and work environment are tidy and free of visually complex elements such as multiple patterns, colors, and visually discordant clutter. Workspace contains only those items needed in the moment; other items are stashed away out of sight.

## TOUCH

All fabric (bed, bath, and worn) that comes into contact with skin is soft and free of labels or irritating, thick stitching or lining. "Soft" shower head settings or warm (not hot or cold) baths are used.

## SMELL
Added fragrance is limited in laundry, body soaps, and other cleaning products. Work or home space has filtered air.

## THREE BODY REGULATION SENSES

Schedules and routines provide a substitute for internal sensory feedback. Deliberately cued and/or learned patterns of behavior mimic missing sensory information.

# TURNING POINTS

*Just as each developmental stage in human life features "typical" physical and psychological changes, so too does the atypical person go through stages, or turning points, in their lives where the "atypical" is expressed and developed.* At each life stage, the typical person has a series of developmental "jobs" to complete. Atypical people usually have the same (and often additional unique) developmental "jobs" to complete and may need to use atypical methods, including learning patterned behavior, supports, or prompts.[3,4,5] *We can gather "clues" at each of these turning points, clues that can assist you in identifying and nurturing your individual strengths as your life unfolds.*

*Your individual superpowers or abilities are unique for you.* For example, I love to dance and have loved moving to music since I was an infant. Dance is satisfying and freeing for me. I feel good about myself and usually the rest of the world when I dance. There are many others who are "better" at dancing than I am, but for me, "dance" is one of my superpowers. Dance contributes meaning and a type of anchor to my life in a way many other activities do not. *As you go through the following pages, it may be helpful to note for yourself aspects of your life or feelings that match the examples or descriptions at each stage of life.* Do not worry if you find overlaps between the senses, because some senses work together and their relationships to each other are complex.

To make this part of the book more fun, I have asked my friend Rebecca, who is a professional book illustrator, to create two characters to guide us: a detective named A. Typical and a scientist named Dr. S. Powers. Our detective and scientist will be showing us facts and example clues at each turning point that you can use to help you find (and note) your personal strengths and abilities or potential superpowers.

# SUPERPOWER TURNING POINTS

## EARLY YEARS DEVELOPMENTAL TASKS

## LIFE STAGE:
### BIRTH TO 3 YEARS OLD

Eating, dressing, engaging with others, speaking, and potty training

## FACTS

### ISSUES RELATED TO AUTISM AT THIS LIFE STAGE

★ Extraordinary brain growth

★ High or rigid muscle tone; frantic or scared affect when being held or nursing

★ Absence or low level of engaging with others such as reacting to smiles, facial expressions, eye contact, pointing, showing, waving at others

★ Pays attention to objects rather than people

★ Persistent preference for solitude

★ Delayed, lacking or regression in speech development

★ Meltdowns or shutdowns

★ Resistance to, or agitation with, minor change in routine or surroundings

★ Crying or irritation with aspects of physical environment: light, sound, new skin sensations or tastes

★ Repetitive behaviors like rocking, spinning, arm or hand flapping, verbal sounds, etc.

# MORE INFORMATION

1. Center for Disease Control (CDC) Developmental Milestones resources[6]
2. In a Different Key: The Story of Autism[7]
3. "Autism Internet Modules" for parents and professionals[8]
4. The ARC resources in your state[9]
5. Early Start Denver Model therapists for infant/toddler intervention[10]
6. Journal article, "Resilience in Autism: Research and Practice Prospects"[11]

Early intervention in parallel with brain development is powerful and can 'train' the brain in weaker developmental areas while identifying and nurturing developmental strengths.

*Dr. Annette Estes, PhD, Director, University of Washington Autism Center, Seattle, Washington*

# RESOURCES

1. Pediatrician, autism diagnosis team, pre-school assessment specialists, behavior training coaches
2. "Autism centers" in your state
3. Non-verbal or non-speaking assessment tools and methods
4. Visual schedules and/or cues
5. Occupational and speech therapists
6. Patterned learning techniques including "chunking" and "task analysis" that use the learner's sensory strengths to provide cues
7. PECS (Pictures Education Communication System)
8. American Sign Language.

" It may be that the highest brain growth periods for humans (before three years old and late adolescence) provide a window in time when brain processes can be influenced. For example, young autistic children who do not look at others faces when communicating may be losing the brain growth opportunity to explore and learn from facial expressions. Should we encourage exploring facial expressions with these children so they don't miss out on that developmental learning? When we can capture a child's attention and make ourselves interesting, young children often respond with joy and delight. "

*Dr. Annette Estes, PhD, Director, University of Washington Autism Center, Seattle, Washington*

## SUPER TOUCH, VISION AND/OR HEARING

Difficulty in toilet training due to environmental sensory overload that stop when:

★ Toilet seat has soft material or is warm

★ Flushing happens when seat cover is down or after child has left the room

★ Light intensity is reduced

★ Toilet time is a part of cued daily routine

★ Learns other basic developmental tasks only when sensory stresses are identified and addressed or incremental steps are consistently affirmatively cued.

## SUPER TOUCH OR SMELL

★ Consistent crying, squirming, rejection of clothing or things like bath towels that stop when:

★ Change to softer material

★ Tags, buttons, snaps, and/or fabric lining or stitching is eliminated

★ Fragrance is neutralized

## SUPER HEARING

★ Startle, cower, and cry or scream for extended time with loud or persistent noise and/or in anticipation of noise

★ Can repeat songs or mimic musical tunes beyond typical developmental level

★ Loves to repeatedly mimic and/or play games with toys/instruments that make sounds

★ Can repeat or "read" story beyond typical developmental level

# SUPER VISION

* ★ Calms markedly with reduced light levels, seeks spaces to play or carry out other activities that have lower light intensity
* ★ Complains and/or shields eyes, squints at light levels that do not seem to affect others
* ★ Seeks out and/or calms when repetitively watching movement of objects
* ★ Consistently looks peripherally at objects or people.

# SUPER TOUCH OR VESTIBULAR SENSE

* ★ Loves repetitive body movement over long periods of time such as spinning, rocking, jumping.
* ★ Likes and/or calms when wrapped tightly in blankets or clothing
* ★ Avoids or exclusively selects specific toy surfaces or food textures

# SUPER INTERNAL BODY SENSES

* ★ Likes or avoids tumbling, trampolines, dancing to music, objects that spin, swing, or twist the whole body in space
* ★ Likes and repeats or avoids activities that require body coordination or agility
* ★ Likes and repeats or avoids activities that use fingers, utensils, crayons, pencils, or tools to make or manipulate things
* ★ Likes or avoids games or activities that involve pushing, pulling, lifting
* ★ Likes or avoids games or activities that involve weight or pressure being placed on body
* ★ Recognizes or does not recognize and/or ask to eat/drink when hungry/thirsty; being tired and need for rest
* ★ Can communicate or does not recognize pain, being too hot or cold, feeling sick
* ★ Can communicate how body feels when experiencing an emotion

# SUPERPOWER TURNING POINTS

## PRE-SCHOOL YEARS DEVELOPMENTAL TASKS

### LIFE STAGE: 3 TO 6 YEARS OLD

Cooperative playing, friendship, recognizing and expressing emotions, sitting still, participating in group activities, transitioning from one activity to another, identity.

## FACTS

### ISSUES RELATED TO AUTISM AT THIS LIFE STAGE

★ Sensory issues resulting in triggered meltdowns and/or agitation with close group contact

★ Decisions about modification or repression of stims that may be seen as disruptive or non-compliant

★ Resists or ignores transitions to different activities

★ Mimics social interactions from media or other people when responding to social situations

★ Hyper-focused interests and/or repetitive behavior

★ Identifying feelings and learning calming routines and environmental mitigation to enable focus and self-regulate

★ Hyperlexia (learning to read and/or complete reading related school tasks early and rapidly)

★ Co-occurring health conditions (see more detail below)

★ Issues from prior life stage

## RESOURCES

1. Pediatrician, autism diagnosis team, occupational and speech therapy and/or developmental coach, pre-school special education specialists
2. The Arc chapter in your area or state[9]
3. How to respectfully talk about disability[12]
4. Parent-to-parent support and networking groups in your area[13]
5. Your state's or area's "Autism Center"

## MORE INFORMATION

1. Visual cues for schedule or multi-step activities
2. Sensory accommodations for daily living to reduce the irritation, intrusion or intensity of overwhelming noise, light, taste, smell, or skin sensation (touch)
3. Assistive aids for communication and sign language or visual cues to offset atypical auditory processing or language development
4. Health care interventions for conditions frequently seen in persons with autism like gastro-intestinal issues, apraxia (an involuntary movement disorder), epilepsy, eating and feeding issues, anxiety; compulsive behavior; sleep disturbance; and attention deficits

Who knew potty training could be so difficult? Lack of potty training became an obstacle to overcome in order for our child to attend day-care and school. We had already been asked to remove him from two daycare programs. We had talked to pediatricians and tested him for allergies and intolerances. Finally the developmental preschool our son attended had a parent support group, and there we learned about potty training "aids" and even a potty training coach. Our son's body did not recognize the impulse to use the bathroom [interoceptive sense], and the room itself presented so many over stimulations that were uncomfortable to him—the flushing noise was especially frightening. The combination of finding out that our son was intolerant to wheat, causing constipation, and the help of a potty training coach with routines, visual cues and bathroom modifications did the trick.

*(Family story of an autistic young adult)*

“ I convinced myself that my child would just 'grow out of it' in time. I don't want my kid to be 'labeled' and suffer the social consequences of that. ”

*(Family stories by parents of autistic children and young adults)*

“ Don't rob your kids of life experiences and support that enrich their lives now and into the future, because you want to protect them from your perception of the social consequences that might result from their autistic differences. ”

*(Advice of two autistic adults)*

# CLUES RELATED TO SENSORY SUPERPOWERS

Clues from prior turning point(s), plus:

## SUPER VISION AND/OR HEARING

★ Seeks play that is farther from noise and/or visual stimulation

★ Complains and/or covers ears/eyes

★ Squirms, moves away, or resists entering space or activity that is visually stimulating or noisy (or when noise or visual stimulation is added)

★ Prefers and seeks visual stimulation that is repetitive, spinning, or includes other types of motion

★ Seeks repetitive video or audio recordings and/or remembers and repeats songs or narrative

★ Does not seem to "hear" instructions or requests until second or third reminder; delayed response

★ Responds more readily to visual vs auditory cues/instructions or vice versa

★ Spots or remembers differences in visual or auditory detail easily

★ Solves puzzles beyond typical developmental stage easily and/or quickly

## SUPER TOUCH

★ Does not like to sit in groups or stand in a line with others. Dislikes being touched by others in play—avoids, objects, or acts out

★ Likes repeated activities where pushing heavy objects, intense touch or body "hugging" is involved, seems to calm when engaged

★ Seeks or rejects (including meltdowns) when entering/leaving shower, swimming pool, new clothing, towels or other situations that involve skin-related sensations (clay, finger paint, etc.)

## SUPER TASTE OR SMELL

★ Spits out, melts down, or refuses food due to texture, taste, odor, or appearance

★ Rejects foods previously eaten but prepared in a way that alters texture or appearance—crunchy vs soft or vice versa

★ Rejects foods previously eaten but presented in a different way, such as on a plate rather than in a bowl, on a plate with other food (including touching other food), garnished

★ Enjoys the same foods repeatedly—restricted food interests

★ Only eats foods presented one at a time or of the same color or texture

★ Places food in specific locations or in a specific order prior to eating

# SUPER INTERNAL BODY SENSES

- ★ Likes and repeats or avoids tumbling, trampoline use, dancing to music, play, or objects that spin, swing, or teeter the whole body in space
- ★ Likes and repeats or avoids activities that require body coordination or agility like catching, jumping, balancing, and skipping
- ★ Likes and repeats or avoids use of fingers, utensils, crayons, pencils, or other tools to make or manipulate things
- ★ Likes or avoids activity that involves pushing, pulling, lifting
- ★ Likes or avoids weight or pressure being placed on body
- ★ Recognizes or does not recognize and/or asks to eat/drink when hungry/thirsty; go to bed or rest when tired
- ★ Can communicate or does not recognize pain, being too hot or cold, feeling sick
- ★ Can communicate or does not recognize how body feels when experiencing an emotion

# SUPERPOWER TURNING POINTS

## DEVELOPMENTAL AND / OR SENSORY TESTING

Autism spectrum disorder (ASD) or sensory processing disorder diagnosis

**LIFE STAGE:**
AT ANY POINT IN LIFE; HOWEVER, 2 TO 9 YEARS OLD IS MOST COMMON.

Girls may have more subtle or masked symptoms that can lead to missed or delayed diagnosis. Adults have sometimes been misdiagnosed with mental illness such as schizophrenia, ADHD, or developmental disability.

## FACTS

### ISSUES RELATED TO AUTISM AT THIS LIFE STAGE

★ Developmental delays and/or atypical behavior especially in communication or social engagement with others

★ Restricted and/or repetitive patterns of behavior

★ Restricted or focused interests

★ Stims, behavior and/or meltdowns that are seen as disruptive by neurotypical people in school, work, community and/or family life.

★ Atypical social behavior that affects workplace relationships and/or ability to attain or retain employment and/or personal relationships

★ Delay in response or "acting out" when asked to transition from one activity or sensory environment to another

★ Does not like to vary from familiar routines

1. School psychologist; physician; psychiatrist; autism specialists with school district or state education department; autism diagnosis teams with children's health care or University health centers

2. Occupational and speech therapists focused on social play, assistive communication, motor skills, self-regulation and sensory differences

3. Center for Disease Control (CDC) Autism resources on diagnosis and development[14] as well as specific differences for girls[19]

## MORE INFORMATION

1. *Diagnosing Autism Spectrum Disorders: A Lifespan Perspective* [15]

2. Adult "self test" for ASD see Neuroclastic.com, a website for and by adults on the spectrum. [16]

3. *Finding Strengths in Autism* [17]

4. *Out-of-Sync Child* and *The Out-of-Sync Child Grows Up* [18]

5. *Understanding Your Child's Sensory Signals* [20]

6. *Navigating Autism: 9 Mindsets for Helping Kids on the Spectrum*, chapters 1-3 [20]

7. Autism Internet Modules for parents and professionals [21]

8. *Finding the Right Autism Services for Your Child* [22]

9. *The Nine Degrees of Autism: A Developmental Model* [23]; Training for neurotypical parents/caregivers related to understanding autistic abilities, differences and autistic sensory experiences

Their daughter was good at mimicking other children her own age, especially in play and social interactions. That all changed when she reached adolescence and social interactions became more subtle and complex. It was not until that time in her life that the parents realized she and the family needed help. Other signs were there, but they had been missed.

**(Client story, late diagnosis young adult)**

"Our child was given an intelligence test. Because he did not talk, he scored quite low. Later he was given a non-verbal intelligence test and scored in the 'average' intelligence range. Different worlds were open to him."

**(Family Story, young autistic adult who is non-speaking)**

These results challenge the diagnostic criterion that autistic people lack the skills to interact successfully. Rather, **autistic people effectively share information with each other**. Information transfer selectively degrades ... in mixed pairs (neurotypical and atypical pairs), in parallel with a reduction in rapport.[24]

Strength-based assessment methods are now available and being introduced to assessment teams and individual professionals.[25]

**NOTE:**
An "Asperger's" diagnosis no longer qualifies a person for many services. Often an updated diagnosis using more contemporary ASD diagnosis definitions is required.

# CLUES RELATED TO SENSORY SUPERPOWERS

The results of autism assessments or developmental and/or sensory testing/observation will indicate "advanced development," "typical development" or differences (often labeled "deficits") in areas of human development appropriate for a typical person at your age level at the time of testing. As an autistic person, *you can gain clues about your superpowers and strengths by asking questions* about which areas of your development are seen as "typical" or "advanced." For younger people these same "typical" or "advanced" results can be used to identify strengths or superpowers that can be nurtured at home or in school. Asking additional questions or reading about how people with these developmental strengths use them in their lives can help you identify potential paths for yourself.

COMING TO TERMS WITH AUTISM OVER YOUR LIFETIME

# "THE NINE DEGREES OF AUTISM" IDENTITY ALIGNMENT MODEL*

## DISEASE

1. Born on the spectrum
2. Knowing we are different
3. Experiencing "disease"

Source:
Adapted from *The Nine Degrees of Autism: A Developmental Model*, Wylie, Lawson and Beardon. Routledge, 2016

## IDENTITY ALIGNMENT

4. Self-Identification as possibly being autistic
5. Exploring identity options and avenues of support
6. Resolution to identify as a person with ASD

## WELLBEING

7. Self-acceptance
8. Creates and accepts a place in society where strenghts are valued
9. Self-mastery, positive contributions and recognition

*Model applies to other neurotypes such as ADHD or dyslexia as well.

# SUPERPOWER TURNING POINTS

## PRIMARY SCHOOL YEARS DEVELOPMENTAL TASKS

**LIFE STAGE:**
**6 TO 12 YEARS OLD**

IEPs (school Individual Education Plans); novice learning of many types of skills; learns about rules and boundaries; begins developing own internal structure and character.

## FACTS

### ISSUES RELATED TO AUTISM AT THIS LIFE STAGE

★ Challenges with communication and social interactions with neurotypical peers including difficulty identifying and understanding neurotypical boundaries, thoughts and feelings

★ Reads and learns facts well, limited comprehension and understanding of neurotypical social context

★ Negative reactions by neurotypical people to atypical behaviors becomes more apparent

★ Shutdowns, stress, and/or anxiety about compliance with neurotypical norms and expectations, about stimming, sensory or speech accommodations.

★ Exhibits restricted, repetitive, and/ or focused interests or patterns of behavior

★ Co-existing mental health challenges emerge such as anxiety, ADHD, depression

★ Masking or camouflaging of atypical behavior including stimming, especially in girls, becomes apparent

★ Mimicking, without comprehension or understanding of context, neurotypical behavior or social communication becomes apparent

★ Issues from previous life stages

# RESOURCES

1. Health care interventions for co-occurring health issues including sensory-related pain.

2. Speech, physical and/or occupational therapy especially for social skills, assistive communication, integration of motor planning and follow through, or other sensory issues.

3. Counseling or therapy with professionals who take a positive, "difference" affirming approach to ASD.

4. Introduction of paid and un-paid age-appropriate chores and/or work experiences at home or in community.

5. Autism specialists in school district or community to assist with IEP goals especially those related to behavior, stims and nurturing strengths.

6. Social organizations and events in your area specifically for autistic children. Introduction to online activities specifically for autistic children such as *Autcraft* version of *Minecraft* video game.[26]

7. IEP advocates through state education departments or autism non-profit organizations such as PAVE.[27]

8. Local parent support groups, like Parent to Parent.[13]

9. "Outschool," an online learning platform pursuing education through exploring focused interests.[28]

# MORE INFORMATION

1. Medical conditions associated with Autism (See The Spectrum. org.[29])

2. IEP parent resources, toolkits and video series

3. National Autism Association, the Autism Society, plus the National Association of Special Education Teachers

4. *Twelve Ways to Incorporate Strengths ... in the IEP Process*[30]

5. *Autism, Intense Interests and Support in School: From Wasted Efforts to Shared Understandings*[31]

6. *Navigating Autism*, Chapters 3 to 7[20]

# CLUES RELATED TO SENSORY SUPERPOWERS

## RELATIONSHIP BETWEEN NATURE OF THE FOLLOWING AND RELATED SENSES

★ Focused interests
★ Stims or repetitive behavior
★ Triggers for meltdowns

## SUPER TOUCH

★ Intense reactions to jostling by others
★ Brushing/stroking of skin or firm pressure is calming
★ Completes manual tasks rapidly

# HOW CAN I ENCOURAGE FOCUS ON IDENTIFYING AND NURTURING ABILITIES AND STRENGTHS IN SCHOOL IEPs?

Ask about "strength-based assessment" (see bibliography) and/or testing reports that include strengths in addition to "deficits" or "developmental delays."

In the "present levels" section of the IEP, ask that observations of abilities, strengths, focused interests, and positive character traits be included in addition to testing and evaluation results.

The IEP "goal" section is another place where abilities, strengths, focused interests, and positive character traits can be specifically highlighted for further development.

Emphasize "creating an environment for success" for your child by asking questions. Ask what the professionals at the IEP meeting feel would create the best environment for success for your child and what that would look/feel like. Often what creates an "environment for success" for a neurodivergent child increases the opportunity for success for many of the other children in the classroom as well.

## CLUES CONTINUED

★ Is attracted to taking things apart and/or putting them back together

★ Intense reactions, positive or negative, to use of clay, "gack," sand, finger paint, glue, etc.

### SUPER VISION

★ Heightened power of observation characterized by consistent recall of visual images and/or details related to those images

★ Easily detects and remembers visual details, patterns and/or anomalies

★ Can express and/or understand ideas and processes through images or showing someone else, more easily than words

★ Responds readily to visual cues versus auditory cues

★ Completes visual tasks rapidly

★ Sensitive to changes in visual environment; needs less "visual clutter" in order to process visual information

★ Draws, sketches, or creates two- and three-dimensional pictures by hand or digitally.

### SUPER HEARING

★ Can easily recognize, mimic, or repeat complex series of sounds, tones or songs

★ Memories or pattern change is consistently identified with sound

★ Calmed by certain types of sound or intensity of sound

★ Terrified or intense reaction to fireworks, fire alarms and other loud noises

★ Does not seem to process/understand verbal directions—limited receptive language skill

★ Marked delay in reaction to verbal instructions or questions—marked delay in auditory processing

# SUPER TASTE OR SMELL

★ Memories or indicators of change are consistently identified with taste and/or smell
★ Easily recognizes and expresses fine distinctions in texture, taste or smell
★ Strong preferences for (and/or preoccupations with) specific types of food and/or preparation; levels or types of fragrances in the environment

# SUPER INTERNAL BODY SENSES

★ Likes and repeats or avoids tumbling, trampoline use, gymnastics, dancing to music
★ Likes and repeats or avoids play or objects that spin, swing, or teeter the whole body in space
★ Likes and repeats or avoids activities or games that require body coordination or agility like catching, running, jumping, balancing, and skipping
★ Likes and repeats or avoids use of fingers, utensils, crayons, pencils, or other tools to make or manipulate things
★ Likes and repeats or avoids drawing, sketching, 3-D art, cartooning, handwriting
★ Likes or avoids things that involve pushing, pulling, lifting
★ Likes or avoids weight or pressure being placed on body
★ Does not recognize or recognizes and/or asks to eat/drink when hungry/thirsty; go to bed or rest when tired
★ Can communicate or is unable to communicate about pain, being too hot or cold, feeling sick
★ Can communicate or is unable to communicate about how body feels when experiencing an emotion

# SUPERPOWER TURNING POINTS

## MIDDLE SCHOOL YEARS DEVELOPMENTAL TASKS

**LIFE STAGE:**
**11 TO 15 YEARS OLD**

Experimentation; building a sense of self; puberty; developing social skills, especially friendship and behavior toward others; increasing competence in skills and areas of knowledge—moving toward mastery. Extraordinary brain growth and change.

## FACTS

### ISSUES RELATED TO AUTISM AT THIS LIFE STAGE

★ Learning calming routines and environmental mitigation to enable or extend focus and self-regulate

★ Social demands and confusion increase through puberty—girls may "fake" aspects of social skills

★ Navigation of school routine and transitions

★ Learning about and practicing self-protection

★ Strategies for coping with and celebrating "being different"

★ Processing and navigation of *both* neurotypical and atypical friendship, social cues, and patterns

★ Processing and navigation of *both* neurotypical and atypical adolescent social situations

★ Hurtful teasing, bullying or being bullied

★ Social isolation as an individual and/or family

★ Opportunity for recognition and mastery of strengths to offset negative social messages

★ Use of focused interests to build a new or new level of skill or ability

★ Use of interest in experimentation and exploration to expand range and types of life experiences

# RESOURCES

1. Social skills competency curriculum in school and/or community; counseling or life coaching specialists; speech therapy; occupational therapy including breaking down of complex skills or executive function processes into bite-sized learning; cognitive behavioral therapy; social opportunities in areas of focused interests or with adults in areas of focused interests.

2. Assistive learning technology that facilitates inclusive communication among people.

3. Mechanisms for student to review written material about themselves before sharing with family or vis-versa.

4. Use of visual or auditory tools (pictures, icons, word cues, cell phone) for schedule, "to do" lists, self-regulation, or hygiene tasks.

5. Beginning strength-based "Transition Planning" as part of IEP which is optional for middle school, useful for self-image.

6. Set IEP goals that include focused interest "project learning" and pre-vocational skills as part of social skills curriculum.

7. "Outschool," an online learning platform pursuing education through exploring focused interests.[28]

8. Parent- or caregiver-guided new experiences and experiments that may build from or add new focused interests. Even though it may be hard to see the connection now, focused interests may eventually lead to lifelong or career-related pursuits.

9. Continuation of age appropriate chores, paid and un-paid work experiences at home and in community.

# MORE INFORMATION

1. *You Are a Social Detective! Explaining Social Thinking to Kids*[32] plus additional social skills resources for youth and young adults from the same publisher.

2. *Puberty and Autism: An Unexplored Transition*[33]

3. *Strengths-Based Transition Planning: A Positive Approach for Students with Learning Disabilities*[34]

4. See also: "Autism affirming testing and language" in References by topic at end of this book.

Our daughter loves water and music. She is smart as a whip. She can navigate electronics very well and is opinionated like any typical twelve-year-old. She retains information and details, is persistent and good at problem solving. She is a snuggler and is excellent at sensing other people's emotions. Learning for her is associated with people and experiences with people. She uses a communication device and the speech therapist who worked with us has made such a huge difference—the difference between night and day!

*(Family story of middle school girl)*

## RELATIONSHIP BETWEEN NATURE OF THE FOLLOWING AND RELATED SENSES

- ★ Favorite assignments or "jobs" that build self-worth, competency, leadership, and/or responsibility
- ★ Recognition for achievements
- ★ Focused interests or curiosity
- ★ Experiments or explorations
- ★ Participation in group or partner activities

## SUPER TOUCH

- ★ Completes manual tasks rapidly
- ★ Understands relationships among and functioning of multi-dimensional objects
- ★ Takes things apart/tears/crunches to calm or promote focus
- ★ Extended pressure on all or major parts of body to calm or promote focus
- ★ Push large or heavy objects to calm or promote focus
- ★ Touching/stroking soft material or skin to calm or promote focus
- ★ Dislikes or reacts disproportionally to physical contact/touch

## SUPER VISION

- ★ Detailed and precise handwriting and/or drawing
- ★ Easily detects visual patterns and/or anomalies including details
- ★ Completes visual tasks rapidly including keyboarding
- ★ Reduces exposure to or isolates self from visual clutter or intensity—creates or prefers tidy environment
- ★ Uses visual spinning or other movement fidgets to calm or promote focus

## SUPER HEARING

★ Makes sounds to release tension or calm especially around or after sound that is irritating or overwhelming

★ Physically (or through ear protection), isolates self from others to reduce noise volume or clutter

★ Uses sounds/music to promote calm or focus

★ Can easily replicate sounds/music/songs

★ Has perfect pitch and/or detects sound patterns and differences accurately and easily

## SUPER TASTE OR SMELL

★ Explores new tastes, food textures or smells

★ Uses oral fidgets to promote calm or focus

## SUPER INTERNAL BODY SENSES

★ Likes and repeats or avoids tumbling, trampoline use, gymnastics, dancing to music

★ Likes and repeats or avoids activities that involve objects that spin, swing, or teeter the whole body in space

★ Likes and repeats or avoids activities or games that require body coordination or agility like swimming, team sports, skateboarding or skiing, ice skating, track, and field

★ Likes and repeats or avoids activities that rely on fine motor skills like drawing, computer use, handwriting, cartooning, sketching, 3-D art

★ Likes or avoids activities that involve pushing, pulling, lifting

★ Likes or avoids weight or pressure being placed on body

★ Is able to recognize and communicate how body feels when experiencing common emotions

# SUPERPOWER TURNING POINTS

## HIGH SCHOOL YEARS DEVELOPMENTAL TASKS

**LIFE STAGE:**
**14 TO 19 YEARS OLD**

Project Learning; individuality; separation; sexuality and competence.

## FACTS

### ISSUES RELATED TO AUTISM AT THIS LIFE STAGE

★ Increasing independence through building life skills or exploring and using supports for such things as personal health and daily living; driving/transportation; managing money and financial support programs

★ Bridging or connecting intellectual skills and mastery to sensory abilities, focused interests, unique personality traits—your superpowers

★ Building employment or career-related skills or interests through experiences, internships, job shadowing, job training, visiting college programs, and/or experimentation with potential paths in life after high school

★ Understanding and practicing personal responsibility

★ Introduction to new experiences and areas of knowledge beyond the home and school environment

★ Experiencing and sustaining social relationships through focused interests.

★ Neurotypical and atypical friendships, social inclusion or isolation and self-worth.

★ Introduction to "autistic culture"

★ Handling strong or unfamiliar feelings.

★ Sexuality and dating.

★ Issues from previous life stages.

# RESOURCES

1. IEP-related "transition planning" that leads to developing community living skills and supports, high school vocational or job experience programs using focused interest areas.

2. Vocational rehabilitation service agencies; job shadowing and/ or internships; summer job skills programs.

3. Testing: Survey of Autistic Strengths and Skills (SAAA); Risk Inventory and Strengths Evaluation (RISE); Values in Action Questionnaire (personal traits)

4. Educational material on student-centered "project learning" and building personal portfolios. Incorporate project learning and personal portfolio development into IEP/Transition Plan.

5. Community/Technical College or University "navigator" or "transition" programs for persons with intellectual disabilities including ASD. Look specifically for pre-admission "skills" checklists as a guide for high school transition planning goals.

6. Before graduation consciously work to build a network of friends to do things with and adults for support. This network is invaluable for life after graduation.

7. Explore community-based service centers and programs for persons with disabilities.

8. Dating and life coaches for persons with ASD.

9. Attorneys specializing in Power of Attorney and Guardianship law for persons with disabilities.

10. State Developmental Disability agency for personal and job supports.

11. Build from focused interests to find paid and un-paid work or volunteer experiences at home and in the community.

# MORE INFORMATION

1. *Autism and the Transition to Adulthood: Success beyond the Classroom* [35]

2. *Project Based Learning (PBL) for Students with Autism* [36]

3. *The Benefits of Focused Interests in Autism* [37]

4. *Love on the Spectrum U.S.*, Netflix Series, 2022 (Emmy award winner)

5. *Making Sense of Sex* [38]

6. *Navigating Autism*, Chapters 7 to 9. Chapter 8 specifically covers pushing yourself to learn in the "growth zone" in high school. [20]

7. *Preparing Transition-Age Students with High Functioning Autism Spectrum Disorders for Meaningful Work* (Identifies seven promising elements of successful high school transition services) [39]

## SUPER TOUCH

★ Stims or calming activities that are connected to or involve touch or variation on touch, such as vibration, physical contact, physical manipulation, etc.

★ Focused interests or behaviors that are connected to or involve touch, pressure, or manipulation of physical objects

★ Favorite activities or school subjects that involve touch or spatial awareness translated into or connected with a vocational or career interest

★ Likes to keep hands busy with activities or subjects that use touch for an extensive amount of time—manipulation of objects, differentiating through touch, use of body in physical activity, etc.

★ Understands relationships among and functioning of multi-dimensional objects

★ Completes physical tasks rapidly

★ Takes increasingly complex things apart and/or puts them together

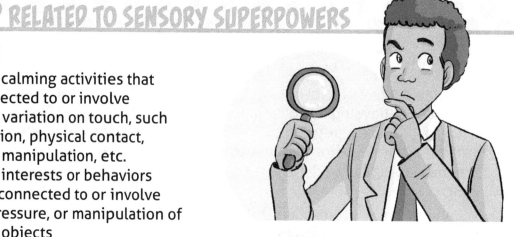

## SUPER VISION

★ Stims or calming activities that are connected to or involve visual activity, spatial reasoning or focus, including use of screens

★ Focused interests or behaviors that are connected to or involve visual activity or visual cues

★ Favorite activities or school subjects that involve visual cues or are visual in nature

★ Subject matter that is conveyed or expressed visually by instructor and/or student

## SUPER HEARING

★ Stims or calming activities that are connected to or involve hearing or sound

★ Intense interests or behaviors that are connected to or involve hearing or sound

★ Favorite activities or school subjects that involve hearing/sound

★ Activities or subjects that are conveyed or expressed using auditory means—verbal, recordings, music, series of sounds, etc.

## SUPER TASTE OR SMELL

★ Stims or calming activities that are connected to or involve taste or smell

★ Focused interests or repetitive behaviors that are connected to or involve taste or smell

★ Favorite activities or school subjects that involve taste or smell

★ Activities or subjects that are conveyed or expressed using methods that include taste or smell

## SUPER INTERNAL BODY SENSES

★ Same as prior life stages.

# SUPERPOWER TURNING POINTS

### AFTER HIGH SCHOOL DEVELOPMENTAL TASKS

The world of work/ community contribution; growing through independence and interdependence; accepting responsibility; mastering skills.

**LIFE STAGE:**
**18 THROUGH FULL BRAIN DEVELOPMENT AROUND 25**

Also called "emerging adulthood" characterized by self-focus, instability, identity explorations, feeling in-between and a sense of "possibilities." [40]

## FACTS

### ISSUES RELATED TO AUTISM AT THIS LIFE STAGE

★ Finding your place in autistic culture

★ Working through barriers (such as job interviews and independent life skills) to, finding and sustaining employment and/or higher education/ technical training that compliments focused interests

★ Experimenting with more independence/ responsibility inside and outside the home

★ Exploring personal spirituality and religious beliefs

★ Mastering life skills or sustaining workarounds/supports leading to independence including participation in state developmental disability programs for adults

★ Making decisions about financial support including SSI or SSDI, guardianship, health insurance including Medicaid and Medicare disability coverage, use of college savings including 529 plans and ABLE accounts

★ Navigating social relationships in both the "typical" and atypical worlds

★ Maintaining and expanding an in person and online social network

★ Issues from previous life stages

# RESOURCES

1.  State vocational rehabilitation services for job search and interview skills, training in interest area and job coach.
2.  Job coaching and skills agencies.
3.  College and vocational program transition, navigator, and disability service programs.
4.  Community-based developmental disability agencies and programs.
5.  Online and/or in person support groups for autistic adults in your area.
6.  Certified therapeutic recreation specialists (CTRS) who work with clients to find community and home activities that fit their client's sensory needs, interests, and abilities.
7.  Private and group counseling, occupational therapy, speech therapy and/or life coaching especially related to adapting to criticism or feedback on the job.
8.  Strengths testing with ASD affirming educational psychology practitioners.
9.  "16PF" and other career interest tests that fit your personal communication style.

# MORE INFORMATION

1.  *Developing Talents*[41]
2.  *The Neurodiverse Workplace*[42]
3.  Testing: *Survey of Autistic Strengths and Skills (SAAA); Risk Inventory and Strengths Evaluation (RISE); Values in Action Questionnaire* (personal traits)
4.  *Life Coaching for Adults on the Autism Spectrum: Discovering Your Potential*[43]
5.  *List of 22 College and University Level Transitions Programs Funded by the US Department of Education*[44]

Using an online survey, researchers compared the perceived benefits and preferred functions of computer-based communication of 291 participants with and 311 without ASD. Participants with autism spectrum disorder (ASD) perceived the benefits of computer-based communication as increased comprehension and control over communication, access to similar others, and the opportunity to express their true selves. They enjoyed using the Internet to meet others *more* and to maintain connections with friends and family *less* than did participants without ASD. People with ASD enjoyed aspects of computer-based communication associated with special interests or advocacy, such as blogging, more than did participants without ASD.

*Source: Research journal article*[45] *(paraphrased)*

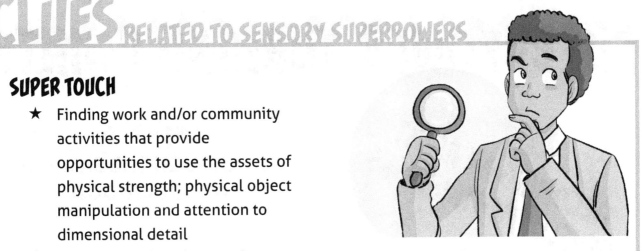

## SUPER TOUCH

★ Finding work and/or community activities that provide opportunities to use the assets of physical strength; physical object manipulation and attention to dimensional detail

★ Avoiding work or community activities that trigger anxiety or loss of focus related to unmitigated touch sensitivity

## SUPER VISION

★ Finding work and/or community activities that provide opportunities to use visual sense assets (like pattern recognition and attention to detail) to cue, respond to or produce work/results

★ Avoiding work or community activities that trigger anxiety or loss of focus related to unmitigated visual clutter

## SUPER HEARING

★ Finding work and/or community activities that provide opportunities to use auditory sense assets like musical or tone memory and perfect pitch to cue, respond to or produce work/results

★ Avoiding work or community activities that trigger anxiety or loss of focus related to unmitigated sound

## SUPER TASTE OR SMELL

★ Finding work and/or community activities that provide opportunities to use taste and/or smell sense assets like taste/smell distinction and ability to detect consistency to cue, respond to or produce work/results

★ Avoiding work or community activities that trigger anxiety or loss of focus in an environment with unmitigated tastes or smells

## SUPER INTERNAL BODY SENSES

★ Finding work and/or community activities that provide opportunities to use internal body sense assets (like fine or large motor skills) to cue, respond to or produce work/results

★ Avoiding work or community activities that trigger anxiety or loss of focus related to unmitigated internal body senses such as a situation where routines cannot be accommodated or are regularly disrupted

# SUPERPOWER TURNING POINTS

**BECOMING AN ADULT DEVELOPMENTAL TASKS**

**LIFE STAGE:
26 THROUGH THE BALANCE OF ADULTHOOD**

The world of maximizing independence

FACTS

## ISSUES RELATED TO AUTISM AT THIS LIFE STAGE

★ Sustaining a framework to maintain lifelong basic life functions: housing, transportation, income, health and mental health support

★ Discovering and sustaining activities that are personally satisfying

★ Struggles with impacts of "autistic inertia"—switching tasks or communicating with others when laser-focused

★ Finding and sustaining a framework of personal emotional support—family, coaching/counseling, partners/friends with similar interests, mentors, community connections

★ Building personal resilience to sustain and regain stability through loss of family members, pets, friends, physical surroundings, disaster, social change or supports

★ Finding your place in "autistic culture"

★ Finding and sustaining personal pleasure, satisfaction, safety, and love as an adult

★ Navigating personal relationships and intimacy with both neurodiverse and neurotypical adults

★ Completing the developmental tasks of adults with ASD (see Nine Degrees of Autism[23])

★ Issues from previous life stages

# RESOURCES

1. Prior Superpowers turning point resources
2. Adult autism support groups (e.g., AANE, Asperger/Autism Network, Autism Self Advocacy Network [ASAN])
3. Attorneys and financial planners specializing in special needs estate planning
4. Other families in your community with ASD family members
5. *Neuroclastic: The Autism Spectrum According to Autistic People*, including nonspeakers[46]
6. Help with depression, anxiety, rejection, PTSD, and shutdown triggers through ASD affirming therapists and other mental health care professionals.
7. Autistic Hoya (blog)[47]: autistic adult self-discovery
8. *Ask an Autistic* vlog[48] (series of videos on YouTube) on autism topics presented by autistic adults.

## MORE INFORMATION

1. *Growing Old with Autism*[49]
2. *Older Autistic Adults in Their Own Words: The Lost Generation*[50]
3. *The Nine Degrees of Autism: A Developmental Model*[23]
4. "Could I Be Autistic?" (webinar for teenagers and adults)[51]
5. Autism Self-test[52]

## CLUES RELATED TO SENSORY SUPERPOWERS

*See prior Superpowers Turning Points*

## EXPERIENCES OF ADULT WOMEN

In a survey of older autistic adults for the book *Older Autistic Adults in Their Own Words: The Lost Generation*,[50] the authors found that adult women identified themselves less often as "heterosexual" than their adult male counterparts; women were more often self-diagnosed with ASD than men, whereas men were more often professionally diagnosed. Women more frequently reported sensory issues and a significantly higher incidence of Post-Traumatic Stress Disorder (PTSD) than men on the spectrum.

# IDENTIFYING YOUR SENSORY STRENGTHS AND ABILITIES

As you read through the life stages in this chapter, you, and perhaps others in your life, likely recognized parts of your life story and some of your personal sensory experiences. You may have highlighted or created audio notes of parts of the text as you read.

**What did you learn about your sensory strengths?**

Some examples of what you might have observed are:

★ I noticed that my "hearing" sense or "auditory" function came up for me in every stage of my life.

★ I know I learn best by "seeing" what I am supposed to do with my own eyes before I try to do a new thing.

★ I think "visually", forming pictures in my brain or on a piece of paper to solve problems.

★ Most of my focused interests have always involved touch.

★ My favorite stims to calm myself or relax involve making my body rock.

★ I noticed all my senses are affected by autism.

★ The most pleasure comes from sorting and organizing objects.

★ I noticed that the ways I stim are auditory (I make noises) or use my vestibular body sense because I love anything spinning, including myself.

★ When I explore my interests, I like to use my visual senses—watching YouTube videos, drawing, taking and looking at photos or images. I remember the information and details the best that way.

Take some time to write or make an audio record for yourself of sensory strengths or pleasures you noticed (if you run out of space here, it is all right to add a loose page of notes or some sticky notes):

1. _____

2. _____

3. _____

4. _____

# IDENTIFYING YOUR POSITIVE CHARACTER TRAITS

All people on this neurodiverse planet have distinguishing qualities or characteristics that describe how they operate from day to day. I refer to these distinctive characteristics here as "traits." Everyone has a set of positive character traits that can be included on their personal list of strengths, contributing to their Superpowers.

Below is a checklist of positive character traits thought to be associated with people on the autism spectrum (see "strengths and abilities" in references by topic at end of book). You can use this checklist to identify your specific positive traits by yourself and/or with others. Once you have identified those traits that apply to you, go back over the list and select the four to six that you feel are your strongest positive traits. We will use these later.

Potential Positive Character Traits Checklist:

- ❏ Hardworking
- ❏ Laser focus
- ❏ Persistent, diligent
- ❏ Uses routine and repetition to build mastery
- ❏ Loyal
- ❏ Expertise in areas of focused interest
- ❏ Straightforward, direct, and honest
- ❏ Enthusiastic
- ❏ Clean
- ❏ Stable and consistent
- ❏ Polite
- ❏ Healthy self confidence
- ❏ Respectful
- ❏ Sense of humor
- ❏ Thoughtful decision-maker
- ❏ Kind
- ❏ Courageous
- ❏ Strong sense of fairness or justice
- ❏ Empathic and caring
- ❏ Flexible in thinking

- ❏ Passionate about interests
- ❏ Independent thinker, objective
- ❏ Innovative problem solver
- ❏ Creative thinker, voices a different perspective
- ❏ Non-conforming, fearless of social judgment
- ❏ Precise and detail oriented, noticing and remembering details others often miss
- ❏ Pattern and inconsistency recognition
- ❏ Maintains routine consistently
- ❏ Exceptional memory and recall
- ❏ Follows a set of social rules that preclude bullying others, judging others, and being swayed by peer pressure
- ❏ Competent and smart, regardless of verbal ability
- ❏ Authentic
- ❏ Lives in the moment
- ❏ Other positive traits you or others have noticed about yourself:

_____

_____

My strongest positive character traits:

1. _____

2. _____

3. _____

4. _____

# FOCUSED INTERESTS

Many autistic people have intense interests: animals, people, songs, objects, videos, activities or subject matter (e.g., memorizing everyone's address in our neighborhood) that intrigue you and give you pleasure to explore, learn about or repeat often. Below is an example from the 2007 study by M. Winters-Messiers of the special interests of twenty-three, almost all male, autistic youth between ages seven and twenty-one:

Themes (followed by specific examples of interests):

- ★ Transportation (airplanes, cars, trucks, trains)

- ★ Music (composing, drumming, rap music, saxophone)

- ★ Animals (frogs, goats, horses)

- ★ Sports (swimming)

- ★ Video Games (role-playing games)

- ★ Motion Pictures (Disney movies, *Star Wars*, vampire movies)

- ★ Woodworking

- ★ Art (anime, cartooning, manga, sculpting)

*Source: Table 2, From Tarantulas to Toilet Brushes: Understanding the Special Interest Areas of Children and Youth with Asperger Syndrome[53]*

As an adult, my son is passionate about travel. Started with a fascination with wheels as an infant and toddler—he would turn toy vehicles over and watch the wheels spin. He turned over progressively bigger things as he got older, like walkers and wagons, and do the same thing. As a young boy it was trains—lying down and watching the wheels rotate at eye level. As an adolescent he remembered details of each trip we took including associating objects in the present moment with similar objects that were seen on a specific trip.

**(Family story of a young autistic adult)**

In the next section of this book, we will be using your sensory abilities and focused interests to identify some of your strengths or superpowers. Before we do that, take a minute to identify your current favorite interests by noting them here or adding to your audio notes.

Right now in my life, I am most interested in the following:

1. _____

2. _____

3. _____

4. _____

5. _____

Have you used any of your interests to build skills or abilities like online research skills or working with or leading others (in groups or clubs) with the same interests? List the skills or abilities you have used when pursuing your interests:

1. _____

2. _____

3. _____

4. _____

# RESOURCES

1. Deweerdt, S. (2020). Repetitive behaviors and 'stimming' behavior in autism explained. Spectrumnews.org

2. Dr. Jed Baker, *No More Meltdowns*, 2012, Future Horizons.

3. *Growing Up Again*, Jean I. Clarke, 1998.

4. Sigman, M., & Capps, L. (1997). *Children with Autism: A Developmental Perspective.* Harvard University Press.

5. Wylie, P., Lawson, W., & Beardon, L. (2016). *The Nine Degrees of Autism: A Developmental Model.* Routledge.

6. Center for Disease Control (CDC) Developmental Milestones resources at https://www.cdc.gov/ncbddd/actearly/milestones/index.html

7. *In a Different Key: The Story of Autism*, Donvan and Zucker 2016, Broadway Books and YouTube video at https://www.youtube.com/watch?v=CjwwFIJdUXc

8. "Autism Internet Modules" for parents and professionals free at https://autisminternetmodules.org/

9. ARC resources in your state: https://thearc.org/;

10. Early Start Denver Model therapists for infant/toddler intervention at https://www.esdm.co/;

11. Journal article "Resilience in Autism: Research and Practice Prospects," 2019, Meng-Chuan Lai, Peter Szatmari;

12. How to respectfully talk about disability at: https://www.npr.org/2022/08/08/1115682836/how-to-talk-about-disability-sensitively-and-avoid-ableist-tropes;

13. Parent-to-parent support and networking groups in your area at https://www.p2pusa.org/

14. National Centers for Disease Control and Prevention (CDC) Autism resources on screening, diagnosis and development at https://www.cdc.gov/ncbddd/autism/facts.html

15. *Diagnosing Autism Spectrum Disorders: A Lifespan Perspective* by Donald P. Gallo;

16. Adult "self test" for ASD see Neuroclastic.com a website for and by adults on the spectrum.

17. "Finding Strengths in Autism" by Rachel Nuwer, May 2021 https://www.spectrumnews.org/features/deep-dive/finding-strengths-in-autism/;

18. *The Out-of-Sync Child* and *The Out-of-Sync Child Grows Up* by Carol Stock Kranowitz. and *Understanding Your Child's Sensory Signals* by Angie Voss, 2011.

19. Arky, Beth, "Why Many Autistic Girls Are Overlooked," Child Mind Institute at https://childmind.org/article/autistic-girls-overlooked-undiagnosed-autism /

20. Grandin, T., & Moore, D. (2021.) Navigating autism: Nine mindsets for helping kids on the spectrum. W.W. Norton & Company.

21. "Autism Internet Modules" for parents and professionals free at https://autisminternetmodules.org/

22. *Finding the Right Autism Services for Your Child* by Dr. Lucas Harrington, PsyD, University of Washington Autism Center, 2021.

23. *The Nine Degrees of Autism: A Developmental Model* by Wylie, Lawson and Beardon, 2016 Routledge.

24. Crompton, C. J., Ropar, D., Evans-Williams, C. V., Flynn, E. G., & Fletcher-Watson, S. (2020). Autistic peer-to-peer information transfer is highly effective. *Autism*, 24(7), 1704–1712. https://doi.org/10.1177/1362361320919286

25. Webinar – "Neurodiversity-Affirming Autism Assessment across the Lifespan: A Strengths-Based Approach" prerecorded; for providers, 3 APA CEs, 3 BBS California CEUs, 3 IL CEUs and 3 WA clock hours) Dr. Sara Woods, PhD Psychology.

26. *Autcraft* version of *Minecraft* video game at https://www.autcraft.com/.

27. IEP advocates through autism non-profit organizations such as PAVE at https://wapave.org/

28. "Outschool," an online learning platform pursuing education through exploring focused interests at: https://outschool.com/about#abl8z6mwqe

29. *The Spectrum* magazine written by and for people on the autism spectrum, quarterly. https://www.autism.org.uk/advice-and-guidance/the-spectrum

30. "12 Educational Apps to Create Digital Portfolios" by J. Nichols at: https://www.teachthought.com/technology/create-digital-portfolios/

31. Wood, R. (2019) Autism, intense interests and support in school: From wasted efforts to shared understandings. *Educational Review.*

32. Winner, Michelle Garcia and Crooke, Pamela (2020) *You Are a Social Detective! Explaining Social Thinking to Kids*, 2nd Ed. Published by Social Thinking plus additional social skills resources for youth and young adults from the same publisher.

33. "Puberty and Autism: An Unexplored Transition." March 2021 https://www.spectrumnews.org/features/deep-dive/puberty-and-autism-an-unexplored-transition/

34. *Strengths-Based Transition Planning: A Positive Approach* for Students with Learning Disabilities, Yeager and Deardorff, 2022.

35. *Autism and the Transition to Adulthood: Success beyond the Classroom* (2009) Wehman et al.

36. Project Based Learning (PBL) for Students with Autism. (2019, Oct 08). Retrieved from https://speedypaper.com/essays/project-based-learning-pbl-for-students-with-autism.

37. "The Benefits of Focused Interests in Autism" by Emily Laber-Warren May 2021 https://www.spectrumnews.org/features/deep-dive/the-benefits-of-special-interests-in-autism/

38. *Making Sense of Sex*, Attwood and Kingsley, 2008.

39. *Preparing Transition-Age Students with High Functioning Autism Spectrum Disorders for Meaningful Work* GK Lee, EW Carter - Psychology in the Schools, 2012 - Wiley Online Library. Identifies seven promising elements of successful high school transition services.

40. Reifman, Colwell and Arnett, Emerging Adulthood: Theory, assessment and application, *Journal of Youth Development*, 2007.

41. *Developing Talents* by Temple Grandin, Future Horizons, 2008.

42. *The Neurodiverse Workplace*, by Victoria Honeybourne, Jessica Kingsley, 2019.

43. *Life Coaching for Adults on the Autism Spectrum: Discovering Your Potential* by Jaclyn Hunt, 2021, ASD Life Coaches LLC.

44. "List of 22 College and University Level Transitions Programs Funded by the US Department of Education" (https://www2.ed.gov/programs/tpsid/awards.html)

45. Intersections between the Autism Spectrum and the Internet: Perceived Benefits and Preferred Functions of Computer-Mediated Communication, Gillespie-Lynch, et al. December 1, 2014 *Issue of Intellectual and Developmental Disabilities* (Journal).

46. "Neuroclastic: The Autism Spectrum According to Autistic People," at: https://neuroclastic.com/ including Nonspeakers (https://neuroclastic.com/category/culture-identity/nonspeaker/ )

47. Autistic Hoya (blog) – *Autistic Adult Self-Discovery* at: https://www.autistichoya.com/

48. *Ask an Autistic* vlog (series of videos on YouTube) on autism topics presented by autistic adults at: https://www.youtube.com/playlist?list=PLAoYMFsyj_k1ApNj_QUkNgKC1R5F9bVHs

49. "Growing Old with Autism" by Rachel Nuwer, March 2020 https://www.spectrumnews.org/features/deep-dive/growing-old-with-autism/ Spectrum Research News.

50. *Older Autistic Adults In Their Own Words: The Lost Generation* by Wilma Wake, Eric Endlich and Robert Lagos, 2021

51. *Could I Be Autistic?* (for teenagers and adults) Webinars of special note University of Washington Autism Center (free) at: https://depts.washington.edu/uwautism/training/uwactraining/

52. Self-tests: https://psychology-tools.com/test/autism-spectrum-quotient or https://www.additudemag.com/screener-autism-spectrum-disorder-symptoms-test-adults/ or https://www.autism360.com/autism-test-for-adults/#start

53. From Tarantulas to Toilet Brushes: Understanding the Special Interest Areas of Children and Youth with Asperger Syndrome by Mary Ann Winter-Messiers, *Remedial and Special Education Journal*, 2007

# 3

# FINDING YOUR SUPERPOWERS

## ONE SENSE AT A TIME

# USING LIFE CLUES TO FIND AND DEVELOP YOUR SUPERPOWERS

In the next two chapters we will take the clues you and/or your family and network of friends and allies have noticed about you and translate them into the Superpowers you can use to build a satisfying life for yourself.

While each of your senses and their associated Superpower(s) is listed individually on the pages that follow, many, but not all autistic people, have more than one interest and a range of strengths related to their senses. A 2020 study of 2,000 autistic children showed that each child had, on average, eight focused interests at a time.[1] Historically these focused interests have often been discouraged, but there is a growing body of research that suggests encouraging focused interests has a lifelong role to play in building a positive outlook, developing areas of expertise, and calming sensory overload.

As you work through each of the senses in the following pages, note those that "fit" for you and your life. You may recognize things you have done or familiar personal interests. *It is okay to mark or highlight those on the page or continue with audio notes.* You may find specific careers or project-based learning opportunities that are exciting or seem interesting to you; *mark or record those, too.* When you are done, you will have some idea of the strengths that are yours or superpowers that are waiting for you to explore and develop in your life.

I use the term "project learning" or "project-based learning" in this section of the book to refer to a specific teaching and learning method in which students learn by actively participating in real world and personally engaging projects. In order to complete a project, students learn, apply, and adapt their skills. Typically, problem-solving skills, persistence, content expertise, and peer relationships are acquired and developed. Project learning can be a valuable learning method for autistic people who are motivated by focused interests. You can leverage that interest to learn or adapt skills you may not be motivated to learn independent of a project in a traditional learning environment. Project learning may also connect students ultimately to satisfying career or community activities.

# TASTE

## SUPERPOWERS

Ability to recall, make fine distinctions between, organize, and replicate taste and texture. This is usually related to food but could be extended to other arenas in life that involve flavor and/or texture. A person may also be able to create new useful combinations of tastes and textures.

# RELATED CAREER OR COMMUNITY CONNECTIONS

★ Chef, including specializations
★ Quality assurance in the food or drink industries
★ Taste tester
★ Food critic
★ Food analyst or technician in food sciences
★ Inventor of new or value-added food/drink products
★ Food bank or senior feeding program volunteer
★ Food server or preparer in a school or a group living facility
★ Caterer
★ Food preparation for online food-related business

# EXAMPLES OF TASTE-RELATED FOCUSED INTERESTS

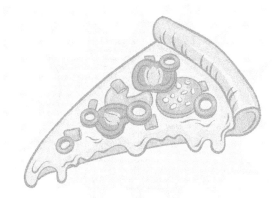

★ Likes to watch *America's Test Kitchen* or cooking competition videos
★ Likes to prepare food or flavor concoctions for others
★ Likes to test recipes
★ Likes to shop for ingredients, help cook or serve food

# EXAMPLES OF TASTE-CONNECTED PROJECT LEARNING OPPORTUNITIES

★ Planning and preparing food at home for a day, week or special event
★ Comparing food prepared in different ways or by different cooks/restaurants
★ Visiting food related businesses to observe food preparation and sales methods
★ Job shadowing a person in the food industry or food science
★ Finding information on food or cooking education programs or websites

# SMELL

## SUPERPOWERS

Ability to distinguish between, replicate, organize, and remember odors based on smell and/or smell memory. A person may also be able to create new or more complex odors.

# RELATED CAREER OR COMMUNITY CONNECTIONS

★ Perfumer (tester and/or mixer of perfume or other scented products)

★ Scented product scientist or inventor

★ Aroma therapist

★ Sommelier (wine master)

★ Odor tester or quality control specialist, evaluating and sampling odors in a variety of industries

★ Criminal investigator specializing in odor/scent

★ Floral arranger

★ Buyer in spice industry

★ Animal trainer for animals specialized in scent identification or tracking

## EXAMPLES OF SMELL-RELATED FOCUSED INTERESTS

★ Collections based on odor

★ Growing flowers or plants with scents

★ Arranging or organizing objects by scent or scent intensity

★ Investigating animals that specialize in scent identification

★ Inventing or playing guessing games that rely on scent for identification

## EXAMPLES OF SMELL-CONNECTED PROJECT LEARNING OPPORTUNITIES

★ Growing and using herbs/spices in food or personal care products for a local farmer's market

★ Job shadowing someone in a scent-related job or industry

★ Identification or experimenting with scent intensity

★ Creating a ranking or identification system for the character of scents among one or more types of flowers or other scented natural objects

★ Creating a story that relies on the "scent memories" of the main character

★ Creating a scent-based treasure hunt

# TOUCH

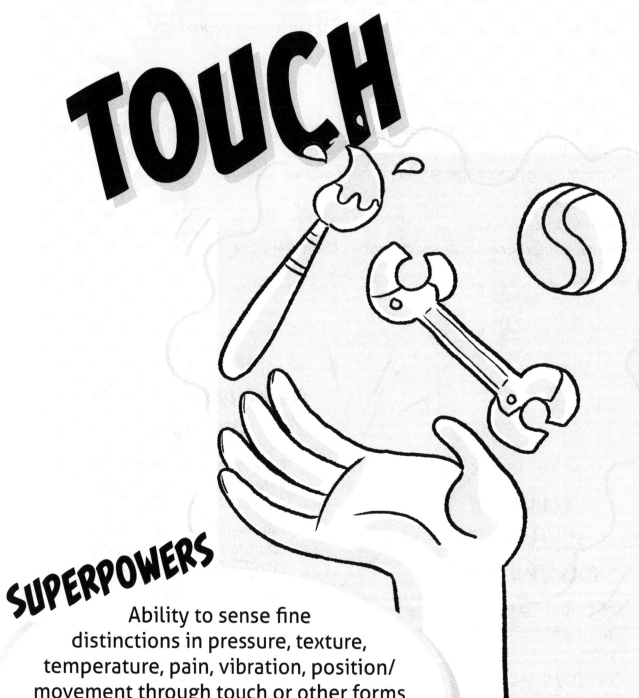

## SUPERPOWERS

Ability to sense fine distinctions in pressure, texture, temperature, pain, vibration, position/ movement through touch or other forms of tactile contact. A person may also be able to recall, organize and replicate these tactile sensations and create new patterns.

# RELATED CAREER OR COMMUNITY CONNECTIONS

★ Master craftsperson or artist in any medium such as paper, clay, fiber, metal manipulation, paint, ink/pencil, and mixed media

★ Massage therapist for people or animals

★ Creator of "learning-by-doing" videos

★ Vehicle mechanic or repair professional for other mechanical devices

★ Installer of mechanical systems for houses, businesses, or industrial plants like plumbing, electrical, solar and heating/ventilating

★ Inventor of products whose primary features are touch-oriented or mechanical in nature—robots, simulation equipment, health related test equipment, animal care products, etc.

★ Mover or warehouse worker

★ Support animal trainer or breeder

★ Farmer—animals or plants

★ Veterinarian, vet assistant, animal caregiver

# EXAMPLES OF TOUCH-RELATED FOCUSED INTERESTS

★ Likes to watch or make videos related to creating craft or art objects, building or mechanical topics

★ Likes to create, collect, or have around them soft, smooth, or otherwise pleasing to touch objects (or the opposite—crunchy, rough, etc.)

★ Enjoys "hands on" creating with clay, paper, Legos, paint, wood, metal, cloth, etc.

★ Enjoys being around and physically interacting with animals

★ Likes to push, climb on, disassemble, crunch, or pound objects—large or small

# EXAMPLES OF TOUCH-CONNECTED PROJECT LEARNING OPPORTUNITIES

★ Building a computer, small robot, or model

★ Building a piece of furniture, clothing, or piece of art

★ Taking apart and putting back together a simple machine, piece of clothing, appliance, or electronic gizmo

★ Making a functional "Rube Goldberg" machine

★ Conducting a "hands-on" science experiment with a video record of the results

★ Building a complete Lego or 3D printed object or series of objects

★ Organizing a toolbox, work area or collection of objects and documenting your work

★ Job shadowing a worker or volunteer in the community who works with things or devices that interest you

# HEARING

## SUPERPOWERS

The ability to distinguish between, replicate, organize, and recall sounds and phrases including pitch, tone, rhythm, intensity, and quality. The ability to create new patterns of sound and/or variation in sound quality.

## RELATED CAREER OR COMMUNITY CONNECTIONS

★ Sound/audio engineer for movies, video games, live and video performances, advertising, cartoons, animation or voice overs

★ Voice talent for animation, cartoons, advertising, video games

★ Individual or group of musicians and/or singers

★ Instrument tuning, construction, and/or repair

★ Music composer and/or conductor

★ Driver of large equipment— construction, warehouse, or emergency vehicles

★ Audiologist

★ Factory equipment installer and repair person

★ Mechanic—small engines to large equipment

★ Language and/or speech specialist

★ Language translator

★ Disc Jockey

★ Music therapist or music instructor

★ Sound/audio producer for video or audio productions

## EXAMPLES OF HEARING-RELATED FOCUSED INTERESTS

★ Listens to music and has favorites that are played repeatedly

★ Knowing words to songs or tunes by heart

★ Playing one or more musical instruments

★ Playing games or videos selected for specific music

★ Knows when sounds are "out of tune" or "not right" with mechanical equipment or musical instruments

★ Recording sounds and/or composing soundtracks

★ Identifies or mimics bird or animal sounds

★ Learns other languages easily

★ Fascinated by radios, stereos or sound systems

## EXAMPLES OF HEARING-CONNECTED PROJECT LEARNING OPPORTUNITIES

★ Recording music you play, sing and/or self-compose

★ Creating a soundtrack for a video or slide images

★ Recording a short story or poem in a language other than your first language

★ Creating an audio collection of your favorite musical pieces

★ Recording and identifying a series of bird or animal sounds

★ Taking apart and putting back together sound equipment or musical instruments

★ Building or wiring a piece of sound equipment or an instrument

# VISION

## SUPERPOWERS

Ability to see, perceive, recall, organize, and replicate fine details or patterns within visual images including the qualities of depth, size, composition, shape, color, light, and surface texture. A person may also create new or variations on visual images.

# RELATED CAREER OR COMMUNITY CONNECTIONS

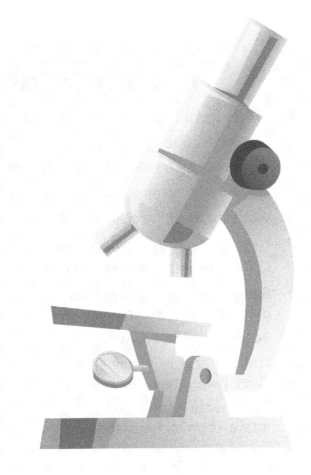

★ Trained observer and/or pattern recognition fields such as police detective, publication/web content editor, scientist and inventor

★ Computer software coder and/or beta tester

★ Traffic, energy, utility, or industrial system controller/ monitor

★ Large equipment operator for construction, agriculture or transportation including pilot and space travel

★ Architectural design, interior design, fashion design, industrial process design

★ Geneticist and biochemist

★ Geographer, cartographer or surveyor

★ Geographic Information System or other database specialist

★ Volunteer or professional in libraries, reused goods outlets, food banks, neighborhood watch groups, Audubon bird counts, citizen science projects

★ Judge for 4-H; county fair; specialty flower, mineral or craft shows

★ Appraiser of art, jewelry, coins, stamps, museum collections or other valued objects requiring attention to fine detail

★ Finance or data analyst in any technical or scientific field of interest

★ Hands-on artistic or building trades worker that require hand-eye coordination skill

★ Maker or production worker requiring a mix of attention to detail, fine motor, and technology skills

★ Visual art creator for computer, publishing, online game, video production, animation, advertising, or educational materials

★ Surgeon, radiologist or other medical specialties requiring attention to detail and/or hand-eye coordination skill

# EXAMPLES OF VISION-RELATED FOCUSED INTERESTS

★ Creating visual art in any medium

★ Cartooning and/or graphic art

★ Creating, organizing or looking at picture albums and/or photography

★ Playing with color in any medium

★ Watching YouTube channels of videos, movies, podcasts, etc.

★ Playing games that involve visual cues or clues

★ Collecting and organizing collections of images or physical objects

★ Building structures or images with Legos, wood, paper, cloth, or natural objects

★ Reading, writing, drawing

★ Website design, coding and/or video game enhancement

★ Documenting collections or interests on social media

★ Video gaming

★ Memory or pattern recognition games

★ Organizing kitchen, pantry or other work spaces

★ Taking apart and/or repairing mechanical devices

# EXAMPLES OF VISION-CONNECTED PROJECT LEARNING OPPORTUNITIES

★ Creating digital or physical portfolios of works or objects you have designed, created or collected; experiments you have conducted; or projects you have done.

★ Creating a video or YouTube channel on a subject of interest to you

★ Creating or copying a work of art

★ Building a physical object like furniture, a model, Lego creation, clothing, baked goods, or a meal

★ Designing, creating, or enhancing a website, Instagram account, blog, gaming server, app, or game

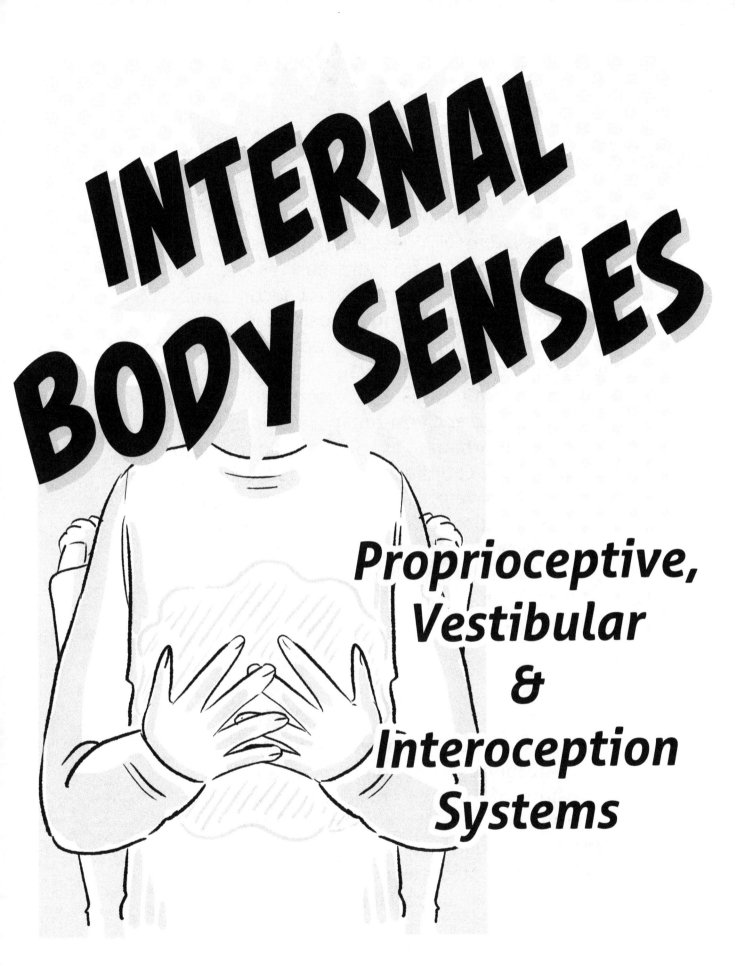

# INTERNAL BODY SENSES

## Proprioceptive, Vestibular & Interoception Systems

# DEFINING BODY SENSES

**PROPRIOCEPTIVE** sense system (or kinesthesia) processes information from the muscles and joints to signal conscious and unconscious awareness of your body position in space (coordination) and enable adjustments in pressure, force, and agility for completion of fine and gross motor tasks. This system works closely with the tactile and vestibular systems to organize sensory information as a foundation for motor planning and coordination. Proprioceptive input can be effective in calming, soothing, regulating, or alerting (from an aroused nervous system resulting from sensory input through other senses).

**VESTIBULAR** sense system responds to motion or change in position of a person's head. The receptors in the inner ear tell the brain what direction and speed the head is moving. The visual and vestibular systems work together to produce visual-spatial awareness.

**INTEROCEPTION**

sense is a human body's internal feedback system that receives body receptor signals and transmits them to the brain for processing into the "feelings" the brain recognizes as hunger, thirst, the need to go to the bathroom, pain, fatigue, nausea, sexual arousal, body temperature, and more. This system also allows us to "feel" our emotions, most of which are linked to physical sensations in our body. For example, anger can be linked to tightened muscles— fists and teeth clench, heartbeat quickens, and face gets warm. The ability to recognize our own physical signals is aligned with our ability to recognize and regulate emotions.

# IT IS POSSIBLE TO GET EITHER TOO MUCH AND/OR TOO LITTLE INPUT FROM ALL OR PARTS OF THESE THREE SYSTEMS.

# SUPERPOWERS
## RELATED TO INTERNAL BODY SENSE SYSTEMS INCLUDE:

★ Quick recognition and response to internal body sensations—getting a drink at the first body signal of thirst—that allows you to maintain your body's well-being and regulate emotion for a high percentage of your waking hours

★ Quick and accurate recognition of emotions from interoception that informs emotional intelligence (the ability to perceive, control, and evaluate emotions in yourself and others). For autistics, studies show enhanced emotional intelligence with other autistics but not necessarily neurotypical people

★ Excellent visual-spatial awareness that allows people to picture shapes or objects in their minds without seeing them

★ Excellent balance and coordination that improve muscle tone, posture and visual awareness when moving

★ Athletic ability

★ Ease in manipulation of objects

★ Hand-eye coordination including rapid, effective/efficient physical responses

## RELATED INTERNAL BODY SENSE CAREER OR COMMUNITY CONNECTIONS

★ Master craftsperson, maker, or artist in any medium: clay, wood, fiber, metal, paint, paper, mixed media, ink, print and/or digital art

★ Textile or fabric design and fabrication

★ Hands-on building trades worker that requires hand-eye coordination skills such as carpenter or home builder

★ Mechanic for vehicles, outdoor power equipment or robotic production equipment

★ Welder

★ Massage or physical therapist

★ Bricklayer or ceramic tile installer

★ Owning or working for a moving company

★ Delivery or warehouse worker

continued ➡

continued ↓

★ Athlete, dancer, member of a precision performance team, mime

★ Working with or raising large animals

★ Race car driver

★ Bicycle, skateboard, snow board, motorcycle sports participant or competitor

★ Trampolinist, areal yoga/dance performer, gymnast, or acrobat

★ Physical education instructor, coach, or personal trainer

★ Maker or production worker requiring a mix of attention to detail, fine motor skill, and technology skill

★ Surgeon and other medical specialties that require attention to detail and hand-eye coordination

# EXAMPLES OF INTERNAL BODY SENSE RELATED FOCUSED INTERESTS

★ Enjoys "hands-on" creating with wood, metal, clay, paper, Legos, paint, ink, mixed media, cartooning, graphic art, etc.

★ Likes "hands-on" manipulation: puzzles, video games, models, blocks, sorting, stacking, and/or moving objects

★ Pushing, climbing on, pounding or crunching large or small objects

★ Wrapping and packaging

★ Exercise programs

★ One or more sports

★ Raising pets or animals

★ Sorting and/or organizing objects or collections

★ Taking things apart and putting them back together

★ Doing laundry, preparing foods, cleaning, sorting recycling, or performing other home or work-related routine-driven physical activities

# EXAMPLES OF INTERNAL BODY SENSE-CONNECTED PROJECT LEARNING OPPORTUNITIES

★ Building and/or creating an art, craft, or digital object or model

★ Construction of a piece of furniture, clothing, or other object or tool

★ Assembling or repairing an electronic piece of technology or mechanical device with lots of parts

★ Job shadowing or interning with a person who does a physically demanding job

★ Job shadowing or interning with a person who does a job that requires excellence in hand-eye coordination

★ Mastering and/or participating in a sport

★ Preparing, planting, growing, and harvesting a garden or agricultural crop

★ Create a physical or digital portfolio of things you have built or created, experiments you have conducted, or projects you have done

★ Keep a written, video or picture journal of things you have done, including notes about what you would or would not do next time you repeat an activity

# USING LIFE CLUES TO FIND MY STRENGTHS

By now, you probably have some ideas about your strengths based on what you know you can already do, your focused interests, and some of the sense-based learning and career options that excited or sparked your interest in the previous chapter. Take a minute to make a written or audio list of the strengths and career/community connections or project learning ideas that interest you most. Feel free to add your own ideas that have not appeared in this book so far. If you need more room, add a loose piece of paper or sticky notes.

## NEW STRENGTHS OR ABILITIES THAT I NOTICED FROM THIS PART OF THE BOOK:

1. _____

2. _____

3. _____

4. _____

5. _____

## CAREER/COMMUNITY CONNECTION OR PROJECT LEARNING IDEAS THAT APPEAL TO ME THE MOST:

1. _____

2. _____

3. _____

4. _____

5. _____

# POTENTIAL AUTISTIC STRENGTHS IN THE WORKPLACE

A number of research studies have identified potential strengths that people with autism can exhibit or use effectively at work. While reports of the employment rate among autistic people varies widely, as the Neurodiversity Movement gathers strength, the more work opportunities there may be. Already progress has been made through advances in transition services from high school to adult life; identification of paths to overcome common barriers to employment; more flexible work opportunities in general; and wider societal understanding of autism. Whether working for others, working as contract employees, or running their own businesses, autistic people bring many highly sought-after qualities to the workplace. The diagram below documents many of the potential strengths of autistic people from existing research.

*Using the diagram (on the next page) and your life experiences so far, write or create an audio list of five potential strengths you personally could bring to a workplace or community volunteer activity:*

1. _____

2. _____

3. _____

4. _____

5. _____

# DIAGRAM OF THEMES AND SUBTHEMES

## SOURCE: "THE STRENGTHS AND ABILITIES OF AUTISTIC PEOPLE IN THE WORKPLACE"[2]

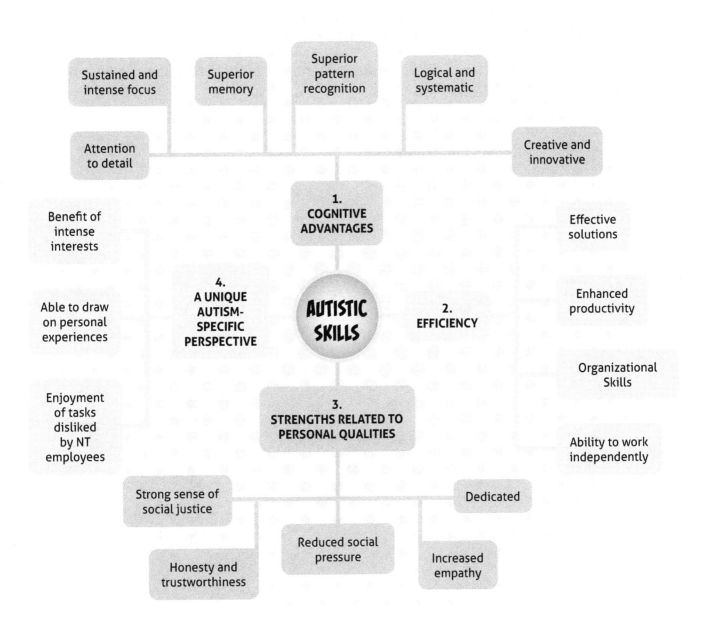

# RESOURCES

1. *Spectrum Research News* Special Report: Autistic Strengths and Special Interests by various authors, 2021 at: https://www.spectrumnews.org/features/legacy-special-reports/special-report-autistic-strengths-and-special-interests/

2. "The Strengths and Abilities of Autistic People in the Workplace" by Cope and Remington, March 2022 *Autism in Adulthood* (Journal)

# CHAPTER 4

# PUTTING IT ALL TOGETHER

Know that you are not alone. Pursue your dreams. If you want something, don't wait and stand by. Tell somebody and find people to help you pursue your dream.

Research it on the internet. Test it out to see if you actually like it—it is not too complex, people won't boss you around, it doesn't involve too much communication with other people and there are not too many parts involved to be successful.

Don't think about all the things that are "wrong" or the people with assumptions about what you can and cannot do. You have strength enough; go to someone else who will not stand in your way.

**(Advice to others from a young man with autism)**

# FOCUS ON DEVELOPING YOUR SUPERPOWERS

## Fighting the "Deficit" War

Autistic people and their families are often bombarded with information and guidance by well-meaning people in government programs, health care, mental health care, and education. This information or guidance is usually about what neurotypical skills and abilities the autistic child/person is lacking—sometimes referred to as "deficits." The identified "deficits" are often described as developmental milestones, skills, abilities, or behaviors that are *different* from the "typical." These practices persist "... despite societal shifts towards **conceptualizing autism as a natural human variation**, rather than a condition to be corrected or cured."[1]

Focusing on deficit interventions versus respect for differences can lead to negative outcomes, including denying people with ASD the opportunity to develop and use their superpowers or self-calming behaviors. Focusing solely on "deficits" can contribute to negative self-image and/or feelings of frustration, hopelessness, or despair. Social isolation, bullying, and withdrawal from or fear of social interaction is common.

These negative outcomes can affect the autistic person, their families, and allies.

It can seem like you and your family are pushing a huge rock up a hill and lots of things are getting in the way, to the point that you feel the top of the hill will never be reached, so why even try?

Research backs up these experiences. Teams—you, your family, and allies—perform best if the members of the team have "psychological safety," which means "**all members** of the team can speak up without being ignored or disrespected."[2] An environment that discounts or prevents one or more members of the teams' contribution markedly decreases motivation and achievement **of the entire team**.

Studies on learning have concluded that all people undergo a shift over their lifetime from **learning most from positive feedback as children and novices in development of specific skills and abilities** to learning most from negative feedback as adults or those who have achieved mastery of specific skills and abilities. Adolescents (ten to nineteen) transition from one to the other with age, mastery, and accomplishment.[3] **Focusing constantly on "deficits" is counter to supporting a healthy learning and emotional environment.**

When I was a kid, people thought I was sick and needed to be "cured." I was removed from class and put in a "safe room" by myself which I really did not like; it felt like a jail cell. In fourth grade I finally had a "box" that my family and I made with things I liked to do inside. I could go there any time I wanted to. It was my version of the "hugging machine" that Temple Grandin made for herself in the movie. All people needed to do was "listen" rather than freak out more around me when I had a meltdown.

*(Memories of a young autistic man)*

*"It is okay to ask for help"* can be a hard message to act on. A lot of autistic kids and adults (and sometimes their allies as well) have accumulated experiences of being ignored or discounted. Asking for help can be daunting, when your life seems so "stuck" or "worthless."

*(Reflections of several young autistic adults, caregivers, and adult allies)*

I am so burnt out from coping with and constantly explaining my autistic differences to the people in the neurotypical world around me. I just want to be me!

*(Personal story of a young autistic adult and repeated by two family caregivers about their experiences)*

Isolation only works if you can experience a satisfying level of joy and the warmth of companionship by yourself.

*(Advice of an autistic adult)*

Focusing on deficits (essentially negative feedback) can deny Autistics their positive childhood and adolescence—hindering learning, motivation, and the opportunity for mastery and accomplishment. Depression is common in autistic people especially in adolescence—ten to nineteen years old.[4]

Would it not be better to think of our children and ourselves as gardens or forests where "the allies" are mature plants who are producing, nourishing, and caring for seeds and seedlings that will turn into all kinds of interesting healthy plants and flowers over time? None of the gardens or forests will look alike, but they each can bring joy to their own hearts and the world around them.

Trying to balance working through, around or past "deficits" while discovering and growing each person's Superpowers requires energy. Fortunately, discovering and growing

Alleviating the pressure placed on autistic people to move toward "typical cognitive functioning" can reduce stigma, promote inclusivity, and embrace the individual.[5] Adopting research frameworks that focus on difference, not deficit, allows the research community to explore meaningful questions that will improve the lives of neurodivergent people.[6]

your Superpowers generates energy, lots of energy, that can be used to fight the deficit war in the neurotypical world. In every phase of life today, families and allies struggle to keep their balance. In every situation you face; finding, growing, and learning from your Superpowers gives you more ammunition.

Individualized Education Plans (IEPs) in the Pre-K–12 education system are a key example of "deficit" focus instead of nurturing strengths. IEPs are completed and followed every year, and sometimes more frequently, for all special education students, including most children affected by ASD.

IEPs are governed by decades-old state and federal laws and regulations which reinforce the "deficit" approach to special education. Testing is required periodically to identify developmentally appropriate "deficits" that are addressed by education goals for the student.

The same testing (along with developmentally appropriate verbal or non-speaking ASD diagnostic testing) also identifies where the student meets or exceeds a "typical child" standard. Identifying and exploring where the child meets or exceeds standards gives some specific clues to abilities and strengths to nurture at home, in the community, and at school combined with the child's positive character traits and intense interests.

Allies like PAVE,[7] autism educational specialists, occupational therapists, and speech therapists can assist families to translate testing into meaningful understandable statements of strengths, interests or abilities to be nurtured.

The study findings showed that having time with autistic friends and family can be very beneficial and played an important role in a happy social life for people on the spectrum. "… spending time with other autistic people was easier and more comfortable … they were better understood by other Autistic(s) … in order to spend time with neurotypical(s) … they had to conform with what the neurotypical people … were used to … Autistic people felt … they belonged with other autistic people … they could be themselves …"[8]

## Social intelligence "differences" vs "deficits"

Is there more than one legitimate form of human social intelligence? Social intelligence has been found to be just as strong in social interactions between people with ASD as between neurotypical people. Where social intelligence faltered for **both** groups was when neurotypical and neuroatypical people communicated with each other. There seem to be at least two forms of social intelligence, not one legitimate form that others lack.[9]

# MAPPING MY STRENGTHS AND ABILITIES

Throughout this book, you have been invited to highlight or record your sensory strengths and abilities, your positive character traits, and your focused interests. On page 84 is a worksheet you can fill in from your notes to map your strengths and abilities; some or all are your personal "superpowers."

If you are stuck, ask for help from someone you are comfortable with. If you need some additional ways of thinking about your strengths and abilities, here are some questions for each heading on the worksheet that might help you fill in your map.

Look through the material in Chapter 2 again. Under the senses you get the most pleasure or comfort from—which of the focused interest areas or project learning ideas appeal to you the most? If something pops into your mind that is not on one of the list(s), that's all right; write it down or make an audio note.

What strengths are associated with the senses you selected (see definition of "superpower" for each sense in Chapter 2)—put those strengths on your map. It is okay if your list is shorter or longer than the three spaces on your map.

 ## My Sensory Abilities and Strengths

What sensory related activities do you enjoy or crave? Think about things you really liked to do or did well as a child. Think about things you really like to do or do well now. What senses do you use when you are doing the things you like?

When you stim, what senses do you use? If you are not sure whether you stim, think about what helps you feel calm. What senses are you using when you are calm?

Where are you the most comfortable? What are the features you most like about your comfortable place? (examples: "it is quiet," "it's warm," "I can be by myself," etc.) What senses are related to the features of your comfortable place?

Based on your answers, which senses give you the most pleasure or comfort to use?

 ## My Best Character Traits

Ask one or two people who know you well to go through the character trait list starting on page 45. Which positive character traits did others think were your best? Do you agree?

It is okay if your positive character traits list is shorter or longer than the three spaces on your map.

 ## Focused Interests

If you are not sure what your focused interests are, you can ask one or two people who know you well to help you identify what you spend the most time or energy doing, talking about, exploring, or asking questions about.

Which of these things gives you the most joy or energy?

Write down the answers on the focused interest list on the map. Do not worry if your list is longer or shorter than the three spaces on the map.

### Skills I Use with My Focused Interests

When you spend time on your focused interests, what skills do you use? A skill might be **talking** about the facts, history, or details of your interest; **finding** and watching videos about your interest; **doing** activities that involve your interest; **creating** art or other objects related to your interest; or **researching information** about your interest. Write down the skills you like using most on your map.

### Thinking Style

Look at the table on page 90. Ask the people who know you well to help you identify your thinking style, and write or record the one or two styles that match you the best on your map.

### Workplace Strengths and Abilities

Look at the picture on page 74. Ask the people who know you well to help you identify your strengths and abilities from among those in the picture. Write or record them on your map. Do not worry if your list is longer or shorter than the three spaces on the map.

If you are stuck, here are some general questions that might identify a strength or ability:

★    How do I like to communicate and have others communicate with me?

★    What do I like best about myself?

★    What do other people like best about me?

★    What do I like best about being autistic?

★    What do I like best about others who are autistic?

*Write your answers on the map.*

*Don't worry if they don't seem to fit in one of the defined spaces.*

# MY STRENGTHS AND ABILITIES MAP

**Strengths and abilities from my senses (pg 44)**

1. _____
   _____
2. _____
   _____
3. _____
   _____

**My best character traits (pg 45)**

1. _____
   _____
2. _____
   _____
3. _____
   _____

**My focused interests (pg 47)**

1. _____
   _____
2. _____
   _____
3. _____
   _____

**ME**

**Skills I use with my focused interests (pg 83)**

1. _____
   _____
2. _____
   _____
3. _____
   _____

**My thinking style(s) (pg 90)**

1. _____
   _____
2. _____
   _____
3. _____
   _____

**Potential workplace strengths and abilities (pg. 74)**

1. _____
   _____
2. _____
   _____
3. _____
   _____

*FINDING YOUR SUPERPOWERS*

# USING MY STRENGTHS AND ABILITIES MAP IN MY LIFE

Among your strengths and abilities are your personal superpowers. Aligning or matching elements of your life with your strengths and abilities provides a foundation for personal growth, personal pride, social connections, and confidence. Depending on where you are in your life span, you may use your strengths and abilities map to guide different types of decisions. Here are some examples:

## USES FOR STRENGTHS AND ABILITIES MAP

| PRIMARY SCHOOL | SECONDARY SCHOOL | TRANSITION TO ADULTHOOD | ADULTHOOD |
|---|---|---|---|
| ★ Individual Education Plan (IEP)<br>★ Building your personal and family support network | ★ Individual Education Plan with Transition Element<br>★ Guide for personal growth<br>★ Life direction exploration or decisions | ★ Life plan<br>★ Higher education or training<br>★ Work<br>★ Social network support<br>★ Community connections | ★ Sustaining personal connections<br>★ Resilience through life changes<br>★ Mastery and satisfaction<br>★ Sharing with others |

*Here are some examples of how strengths and abilities can influence life decisions and the quality of your life:*

I have worked for years with four to six adults whose family caregivers have died, and they now live in a group home together. Most of the adults are older with ASD. One older man loves to be around people. He enjoys singing "Happy Birthday" and organizing objects. I realized that there are lots of things he and others would enjoy doing that the staff does for the residents now. I can see that we could connect him with places in the community where he would have an opportunity to be around other people. His face always lights up and he is so proud when he finishes logically organizing things. He might really like being responsible for putting away the clean dishes from the dishwasher or setting tables at home. He might also get a kick out of stocking or realigning shelves in a grocery store. Combining things he likes doing would be a dream responsibility for him. I can imagine him greeting people at a restaurant, being responsible for the tableware, and singing "Happy Birthday" to diners in one of those restaurants where the staff serve dessert and sing for customers. It would fit him to a "T." He might also enjoy doing something like that at our senior center, which is close by.

His life would be changed, and so would our work as caregivers. Rather than doing things for the residents that they could do for themselves with a little guidance, it would give us a chance to do things *with* the residents that would make a big difference in their lives and how they feel about themselves. I would feel better about my work as well.

**(Story from an adult group home professional caregiver)**

Our adult son has loved to make art, learn about art, and be around art all his life from the time he was in elementary school and surprised us by creating very complex pieces of 3-D art. His artwork is phenomenal. He would probably be able to sell it, but we don't have the energy to do that right now. He is not a savant like all those shows they have on TV these days. Society seems to define "success" for a person on the spectrum as a life like Temple Grandin or the television program *The Good Doctor*.[10] Not everyone on the spectrum is the same, so "success" looks different for every person, and most people don't understand that. I get tired of being around people who seem to disregard, don't have time for or "think less" of, those who don't fit their preconceived idea of "success." It's draining. All my son wants is "a place to live with someone who loves him." Right now, he loves making art and volunteering at the local art center. He texts in full sentences, but he does not talk, and that can be a hurdle when he is out in the community. In high school, he liked and excelled in shop class. In middle school he drew and painted, loved music and dancing. His teachers used his interest in the American flag to integrate him into his middle school the first year. He worked on a painted mural project in middle school that he loved. He seems happy and confident now as an adult and does not feel the need to be "busy" all the time.

**(Family story about a young man more affected by ASD)**

# PUTTING IT ALL TOGETHER

This section of the book will provide one path (certainly not the only path) that can be followed to grow your personal strengths into Superpowers in a way that sustains your life and brings fulfillment.

We will be learning a pattern and then expanding on that pattern. Essentially, we will be creating a set of building blocks— that support the use of your Superpowers. We begin with building blocks commonly learned at early ages of life and expand on that foundation as a person matures. If you are older, you may need to experience or adapt the earlier building blocks to move forward.

## The Building Block Sequence

**Novice Learning of a Skill** — Breaking down what you want to learn into bite-sized pieces. Individual pieces may need to be modified with sensory mitigation, where needed, to avoid triggering sensory overload. Learn bite-sized pieces of something new, one at a time or in smaller chunks through repetition. You can go through the series of steps aided by cues based on your preferred thinking style—such as visual cues, like pictures or drawings or symbols, for each piece in the sequence. Novice learning should emphasize positive feedback at each attempt.

**Mastering a Skill** — Repeating what you want to learn every day for thirty to ninety continuous days (or more) until you have the pattern down.

**Making a Plan, Starting with "To To" Lists** — Make a list of what you want to do, starting with a shorter increment of time and moving on to longer time periods, as mastered. Review the previous list, celebrating what was accomplished, before coming up with a new plan—emphasize what is accomplished or done well each time. Lists may have a large proportion of overlap in the beginning.

**Making a Project Plan** — Use what you mastered about "making a plan" to create a step-by-step plan for a project related to one of your focused interests.

**Making a Business or Life Plan** — Use what you mastered in project planning to create a one-page business, career or life plan that reflects your Superpowers and focused interests.

**Your Superpowers may change, or be expressed differently, in different life stages so this sequence can be repeated as needed.**

## — ONE METHOD —

**APPLYING LEARNED SKILLS TO YOUR LIFE—MAKING A BUSINESS OR LIFE PLAN**

**APPLYING LEARNED SKILLS TO YOUR LIFE —MAKING A PROJECT PLAN**

**APPLYING LEARNED SKILLS TO YOUR LIFE—THE "TO DO" LIST**

**MASTERING A SKILL FOLLOWING NOVICE LEARNING RELATED TO AN INTEREST OR SUPERPOWER**

**NOVICE LEARNING OF A SKILL RELATED TO AN INTERST OR SUPERPOWER**

Other strategies—used individually or together—for lifelong learning by adults and young adults include:

1. "Task Analysis" with or without cues to facilitate learning of new skills plus one or more of the following methods used in occupational therapy:

   ★ Inquiry or project-based learning

   ★ Scaffolding: "I do, we do, they do"

   ★ "Backward and forward chaining" of incremental steps in a task

2. Participating in a transition program post-high school: Find these programs in your state or region at ThinkCollege.net and/or search for IPSE programs for Autism.

3. Skills and interests surveys coupled with a person-centered plan that includes a "circles of support" element. See example at https://portal.ct.gov/-/media/DDS/FactSheets/ifs_pcp.pdf.[11] Two life skills assessment tools are Assessment of Functional Living Skills (AFLS) including independent living and Essentials for Living.[12]

4. You might consider using the services of a psychologist, life coach, and/or occupational therapist specifically trained in neurodiversity-affirming assessment and/or strength-based methods.

# NOVICE LEARNING

## Breaking Learning Down into Bite-Sized Chunks

Inspired by what you now know about your Superpowers, pick something you want to learn. It might be based on your focused interests, for example, or a life skill that will help you exercise a Superpower. Doing something that is simpler first will help you have more confidence as you move forward.

Ask someone to help you break what you want to learn into discrete steps, if needed, or find a resource that breaks what you want to learn into steps for you (a video, an online "how to" guide, a book or article at the library, etc.)

Create, or ask someone else to create, a simple list of the steps with visual, audio, or tactile cues for each step depending on the "thinking style" that works best for you.

## Finding and Using Your Natural Method of Information Processing or "Thinking Style"

If you do not already know, finding out how you process information best can be done in several ways including testing, matching the descriptions of the thinking styles to your own self-knowledge, or working with a specialist to uncover your natural thinking style. Using your natural thinking style—photo-realistic visual thinker; spatial visualizer or pattern thinker; and auditory thinker—to create cues or present information, can make learning new things easier.[13] In addition, some people learn or organize information more easily by "physically doing" than visualizing or talking about a subject. I call this the "hands on" thinking style. In this case, cues might be physical movements or physical tasks numbered and learned in order, "first and then, second and then," etc.

When using cues to learn, sometimes you need to modify one or more steps by identifying sensory mitigation to avoid triggering sensory overload. For example, a learning step that creates a lot of sound or causes your skin to come into contact with cold, slimy, or rough materials may need to be modified so that it's comfortable to learn and there are no unnecessary blocks to learning.

## Making the Process of Mastery Yours:

Observe what works for you when you learn best: the environment you are in; the thinking method or style you use; when your brain absorbs knowledge best (right after you sleep or exercise, for example); how often you need breaks or calming activity; when you know you have mastered something (for example, when you can "teach" it to someone else or when you can do what you are learning without any or few memorized cues). Once you know how you learn best, you can apply that method again and again as you move forward in your life.

| AUTISTIC THINKING STYLE | DESCRIPTION | INFORMATION PROCESSING FORMAT |
|---|---|---|
| Photo-Realistic Thinker | Combines bits and pieces of pictures in the mind to form ideas or theories. | Pictures and photographs |
| Spatial or Pattern Visualizers | Combines visual spatial relationships or patterns and location information in the mind to form ideas or theories. | Visuals—graphics and pictures combined with text for detail |
| Auditory Thinker | Listens and processes language or sounds in the mind to form ideas or theories. | Listening and processing of language and other forms of auditory information |
| "Hands on" Thinker | Examines, manipulates, orders, or combines physical objects and components using this sensory information to form ideas or theories. | Information processed through tactile experiences |

Source: Adapted from *The Autistic Brain*,[13] Augmented with "Hands on" Thinker described in text.

# MASTERING

Doing what you want to learn every day, **continuously**, for thirty (or sixty or ninety) days.

**Now that you have –**

★ Selected something you want to learn,

★ Broken it down into bite-sized pieces modified, when necessary, to avoid sensory triggers, and

★ Created a simple set of step-by-step cues reflecting your preferred thinking style,

**What comes next is *practicing* –**

★ Start with one or two cued steps and add more as those steps become easier.

★ Practice **every day** for 30 or 60 or more days (if you miss a day, start the count over) until the pattern of behavior can be accomplished independently with minimal cues.

*Congratulations! You have mastered the skill, behavior, or routine you wanted to learn.*

**Neurotypical examples of mastery through practice:**

★ *Learning a new vocabulary word* – 17 repeated exposures to the word

★ *Being able to recall a name or word* – actively use 30 times

★ *Create a habit* – 21 days of repetition to create a habit and 90 days to integrate a habit into your life

★ *Create a muscle memory* – 1,000 to 30,000 repetitions depending on complexity of muscle memory task

★ *If it takes ten repetitions to learn a piece of music,* then it takes 50% more (or five more repetitions) to master that same music.

★ *Mastering a new skill* – 6 months or 20 hours.[14]

★ *10,000 hours and a good teacher to master complex skills* such as software coding or playing the violin.[16]

**Neuro-atypical examples of mastery through practice:**

★ Declarative memory is a strength for many people with autism, and it plays a key role in learning.[17] Declarative memory, or explicit memory, includes recall of factual information, previous experiences, details, and concepts.

★ Declarative memory (patterns, scripts, events, details, etc.) may also explain why autistic people are sometimes quicker to accomplish certain types of tasks or recall facts or details than neurotypical people.[18]

★ Little research has been done on the variation in learning and repetition between neurotypical and atypical persons when learning or mastering various skills or material. It is possible, that autistic people, who often have an exceptional ability to focus, may learn or master skills or material at the same or faster rate than the neurotypical in areas of special interest and/or using their Superpowers. Future research may or may not bear this out.

# MAKING A PLAN

## Start with a "To Do" List

Make a list of what you want "to do," starting initially with a shorter increment of time (say one day or the afternoon) and moving on to longer time periods (say a week), as you master making the "to do" list and accomplishing the tasks you've laid out for yourself.

When the time period is over, review what was accomplished. Say you started with a "to do" list for Monday; review what was accomplished on Monday before coming up with a new "to do" list for Tuesday. Emphasize what is accomplished or completed each time. In the beginning, your "to do" lists may have a lot of repeated items or actions. You are **establishing a pattern** by planning what you want to do, following your plan, and assessing how you did before you go forward with the next plan.

As you move forward with using a "to do" list, eventually the "routine" items can fall off the list and only the things that are unique to your day (or week) would be listed. For example, your Monday list might include the three assignments you need to do for your classes, a trip to the swimming pool after school, reviewing what you accomplished on Monday, and creating your "to do" list for the next day. All of the routine tasks might only be listed as one item or not at all.

### Example of a "To Do" List for Monday:

- ❏ Get out of bed
- ❏ Get ready for the day
- ❏ Catch the bus to school
- ❏ Put my things away and get ready for my first class
- ❏ Attend three morning classes
- ❏ Eat lunch
- ❏ Attend two afternoon classes
- ❏ Finish a calming activity twice in the morning and twice in the afternoon
- ❏ Ride the bus home
- ❏ Eat a snack
- ❏ Do homework
- ❏ Have dinner
- ❏ Do something fun
- ❏ Go to bed
- ❏ Review what I accomplished on Monday
- ❏ Make a "To Do" list for Tuesday

# MAKING A PROJECT PLAN

## Convert to a Project Plan with Steps

Use what you mastered about making a plan for yourself by using "To Do" lists to create a step-by-step plan for a project. It might be easiest to start with a project that is related to one of your focused interests or passions.

The general idea is to include steps involved in designing your project, assembling all the materials for your project design, figuring out the steps you need to follow to complete the project, and then cleaning up and documenting what you did and learned.

At first your project plan can be fairly general and/or simple, and over time it can become more detailed, including such things as exploring alternative designs, tools, and methods, financing, and finding the resources you need. There are software programs and apps that can be used, if desired, when projects become more complex.

One resource for developing a project plan related to a focused interest is "Outschool," an online learning platform pursuing education through exploring focused interests.[19]

Project plans give you experience in organizing and working with others. You can use projects to learn skills that will be useful when you pursue your focused interests or grow and use your Superpowers. Project learning is a great tool to use in middle and high school as you earn credits for graduation and assemble a physical or digital portfolio of projects that you can use to show others what you have learned and your talents.

### Example of a Project Plan:

**Project name: Create a display of my collection**

1. Design: Draw or find a picture of what I want the display to look like.

2. Collect the materials for the project:
   - ★ Make a list of materials including numbers and sizes, if needed
   - ★ Find all the materials and put them in my project box
   - ★ Find the tools I will need

3. Decide where the collection display will go.

4. Ask someone to help me put together any parts of the display project I don't know how to do— or find an internet video, book or other resource.

5. Assemble the display.

6. Place the display where it will go.

7. Arrange my collection in or on the display.

8. Clean up and put tools back where they go.

9. Take pictures to share

# MAKING A BUSINESS, CAREER, OR LIFE PLAN

The centerpiece of this book is about living a fulfilling life over the entire course of your lifetime. Thinking about the quality of your life and finding a path that gets you there—being satisfied with **YOURSELF**, pursuing your interests, enjoying the company and companionship of friends and family, finding ways to give back to your community, being healthy, and being your best self.

For each person—atypical or typical—the contents of a fulfilling life will be unique to them. The "job" of being an adult is to create your best life. Everyone must do this for themselves—with help along the way.

## Converting to a Business (or Life) Plan

Use what you mastered in project planning to create a one-page business, career, and/or life plan that reflects your Superpowers, passions or focused interests. These tools work best if you review them at least once a year—noting your progress and making any needed adjustments.

You can use the example templates I have provided below, or you can find one or more that you prefer online or by asking others. Other life planning resources may be found by searching the phrase "Person-Centered Planning." Additional tools can be found at *LifeCourse Nexus*, an online resource of the University of Missouri.[20]

## Find What Works Best for You and Your Superpowers

★ Write down (or have someone else transcribe) the first thing that comes to your mind when you use the templates for the first time. Use the Superpowers you have identified for yourself and focused interests as a guide.

★ Your first attempt may not be "great," but it will improve over time.

★ Before you revise your plan, take some time to remember what you have accomplished—what went well and what you learned. Give yourself some "grace" and recognition for what you have done, no matter "how" you did it.

★ Revise your plan on a regular basis— once a year, once a quarter, whatever helps you find the best way to use your Superpowers (and focused interests).

## Components of a Life Plan:

1. Friends and family

2. A Home

3. Financial Support

4. Personal Support

5. Social Support

6. Health

7. Work and/or community engagement

8. Spiritual life

9. Pursuing interests

10. Using and sharing my superpowers

11. Emergencies and problems

## Components of a Business Plan:

1. Name of your business and plan year

2. State your business's service(s) or product(s)

3. Overall business goals for the year

4. State your customer and/or sales goals for the year (use specific numbers or ranges)

5. What knowledge or skills do you want to expand or learn to support your business?

6. What marketing methods will you use to meet your customer or sales goals (be specific)?

7. What business administration and paperwork goals do you have for the year?

8. What are your business's financial needs, and how will they be financed?

9. Does your business need a backup plan if things go wrong?

**NOTE:** Before you begin each year's business plan, it's a good idea to see how the business did in all areas compared to your plan for last year. Did you meet your goals? Did circumstances change that you need to consider in the new year? Allow yourself at least three years to become profitable; don't be discouraged!

# SHARING YOUR SUPERPOWERS

## Now That You Know You Have Them, Share Them!

Sharing your Superpowers, focused interests and projects is a great way to connect with others who may share your interests, want to employ you, or learn what you know.

In the "Nine Degrees of Autism"[21] identity alignment model, the last developmental segment is "well-being." "Well-being" includes self-acceptance, mastery, and creating a place in society where your strengths are valued and recognized. Sharing can give people confidence in their own worth and the value of their contributions to the community—helping to create that sense of wellbeing.

There are many ways to share. Pick what you are most comfortable with and find an ally to help you, if needed.

Here are some examples of ways to share.

## Examples of Ways to Share Your Superpowers:

★ Online in personal, neurodiverse, or neurotypical group spaces – websites, blogs, Instagram, social media, podcasts

★ YouTube channel video and/or audio files

★ Visual Art collection – Instagram, WhatsApp, CaFE (CallforEntry.org)

★ Audio collection – Instagram, podcast or WhatsApp

★ Use RecRoom[22] Social App to connect with others

★ Displays in your spaces – home and work or community

★ Share with employers, potential clients, mentors or coaches through building personal or special interest-based physical or digital portfolios

★ Pictures – displayed physically or projected digitally

★ Use something you have made as gifts, cards, or seasonal displays

★ Contribute to industry or club events associated with your Superpowers or focused interests

★ Contribute to community events – county fairs, art exhibits, school, or church-based fairs/events

★ Market yourself and your abilities – through agents, copy writing, using trusts, or ABLE accounts

★ Use your superpowers to do or make something for your caregiver(s) or allies in appreciation for what they do for you.

# RESOURCES

1.  Reframing Professional Language Around Autism, Bulluss and Sesterka Psychology Today June, 2020.

2.  Google Operations Research 2019, https://academy.nobl.io/google-high-performing-teams/

3.  Zhuang, Feng and Liao, Want More? Learn Less: Motivation Affects Adolescents Learning from Negative Feedback, January 2017 *Developmental Psychology*.

4.  Prevalence of Depressive Disorders in Individuals with Autism Spectrum Disorder (ASD): A Meta-Analysis, *Journal of Abnormal Child Psychology*, January 2019, by Hall, Hudson, and Harkness.

5.  Bolis, Balsters, Wenderoth, Becchio, & Schilbach, (2017) Beyond Autism: Introducing the Dialectical Misattunement Hypothesis and a Bayesian Account of Intersubjectivity, *Psychopathology* (Journal) .

6.  Kapp, Gillespie-Lynch, Sherman, & Hutman, (2013) Deficit, difference, or both? Autism and neurodiversity, *Developmental Psychology* (Journal).

7.  PAVE at https://wapave.org/

8.  From 'I never realized everybody felt as happy as I do when I am around autistic people': A thematic analysis of autistic adults' relationships with autistic and neurotypical friends and family by Crompton, et al, *Autism* (journal), Sage, 2020

9.  Diversity in Social Intelligence Research University of Edinburgh, U.K. Watson, Crompton, et al. 2021 Video of findings: https://www.youtube.com/watch?v=dEvg4tbiEhU. Research website: http://dart.ed.ac.uk/research/nd-iq/.

10. *The Good Doctor*, ABC six season medical drama, 2017–2022.

11. Skills and interests survey coupled with a person-centered plan that includes a "circles of support" element. See example at https://portal.ct.gov/-media/DDS/FactSheets/ifs_pcp.pdf.

12. Two life skills assessment tools are Assessment of Functional Living Skills (AFLS) including independent living at https://functionallivingskills.com/ (Partington and Mueller) and Essentials for Living at https://essentialforliving.com/about-us/ (McGreevy)

13. *The Autistic Brain*, Grandin and Panek 2014.

14. Visual cues list at the Autistic Awareness Center https://autismawarenesscentre.com/visual-supports-best-way-use/

15. *Harvard Business Review, Weintraub, Nov 29, 2012; Josh Kaufman, TEDx March 14, 2013*

16. *Outliers*, Malcolm Gladwell, 2008

17. *Powerful memory system may compensate for autism's deficits* Ullman and Pullman, March 2015

18. Reading comprehension 2004; distinguishing differences or patterns in rapid presentations of data 2012 and 2020 ; pitch and sound accuracy and recall 2005; mentally manipulating objects 2016 and 2017) cited in Finding Strengths in Autism, Rachel Nuwer, May 2021, *Spectrum Research News* at https://www.spectrumnews.org/features/deep-dive/finding-strengths-in-autism/ .

19. "Outschool," an online learning platform pursuing education through exploring focused interests at: https://outschool.com/about#abl8z6mwqe

20. Additional life planning tools can be found at LifeCourse Nexus, an online resource of the University of Missouri at https://www.lifecoursetools.com/ .

21. *The Nine Degrees of Autism: A Developmental Model* by Wylie, Lawson and Beardon, 2016.

22. RecRoom social application at https://recroom.com/

# GLOSSARY

## 529 COLLEGE SAVINGS PLANS AND ABLE (ACHIEVING A BETTER LIFE EXPERIENCE) SAVINGS ACCOUNTS

State government-established tax-advantaged savings plans. 529 College saving plan assets may be rolled over into an ABLE account for a person with disabilities who does not attend a college or higher education program. Research and get help in deciding whether to participate in one or both of these saving programs.

## ADHD OR ADD

Attention deficit hyperactivity disorder (ADHD) or attention deficit disorder (ADD) is a neurodevelopmental disorder that is chronic and includes attention difficulty, hyperactivity and impulsiveness (acts without thinking about potential results). Often begins in childhood and persists into adulthood. Can be co-occurring with autism spectrum disorder along with other physical and mental health conditions. Symptoms are different for boys and girls. Most research has been conducted with boys.

## ALLIES

A person or group who is associated or united with an autistic person in an affirming way working toward a common goal.

## APPLIED BEHAVIORAL ANALYSIS (ABA) THERAPY

A therapy based on the science of (primarily neurotypical) learning and behavior. Positive reinforcement is used along with understanding what happens before undesirable behavior occurs and the natural consequences that come from the behavior.

## ASPERGER'S SYNDROME

The historical name of a developmental disorder on the autism spectrum that is characterized by higher-than-average intellectual ability coupled with impaired social skills and restrictive, repetitive patterns of interests and activities. Asperger's is no longer recognized as a specific named diagnosis.

## AUTISM (ASD) DIAGNOSIS

A determination, usually written, by medical and/or mental health specialists that a person meets the DSM-V diagnostic criteria for Autism Spectrum Disorder (ASD). Diagnosis may occur at any age but is most common for a young child. See definition of Autism Spectrum Disorder.

## AUTISM SPECTRUM

The range in severity of impact on individuals from autism. There are three medically defined levels (DSM-V) ranging from people who have difficulty initiating social interactions and organizing/planning their daily activity (level 1) to people who limit social interaction to narrow, focused interests and have frequent restricted/repetitive behavior (level 2), to people who are severely impacted in verbal and non-speaking social and communication skills and have great difficulty in changing activities or focus (including people who are non-speaking).

## AUTISM SPECTRUM DISORDER (ASD)

As defined by health care professionals, a developmental disorder that affects communication and behavior. Can be diagnosed at any age, but symptoms often appear in the first three years of life. Symptoms can manifest differently in boys and girls. Historically most research has been conducted with boys. ASD was defined in 2013 by the American Psychiatric Association in its *Diagnostic and Statistical Manual of Mental Disorders* (DSM) as having three levels, each level including specific primary symptoms. Not all families, individuals affected by autism, or allies are comfortable with the existing definition.

## CO-OCCURRING HEALTH OR MENTAL HEALTH ISSUES

Health or mental health issues which have higher rates of occurrence among people with autism. ADHD, anxiety, and depression are the most common co-occurring mental health issues. The most common health conditions are gastrointestinal problems (such as chronic constipation/celiac disease, abdominal pain, acid reflux and bowel inflammation), apraxia (an involuntary speech and motor planning condition), epilepsy, eating issues, and disrupted sleep.

## COGNITIVE BEHAVIOR THERAPY (CBT)

Focuses on the connection between thoughts, feelings, and behaviors. It is widely used to treat a variety of mental health (including anxiety and depression) and substance abuse issues.

## DECLARATIVE MEMORY

A type of long-term conscious memory, also known as explicit memory, that involves recall of factual information, previous experiences, details, and concepts.

## DEVELOPMENTAL DISABILITIES ADMINISTRATION (DDA)

A state and federal public agency that provides services and supports to persons with disabilities in communities around the country to promote individual worth, self-respect, and dignity.

## DEPARTMENT OR DIVISION OF VOCATIONAL REHABILITATION (DVR)

A state and federal public agency that provides services and supports to persons with disabilities who want to work but experience barriers to employment due to physical, sensory, or mental disability.

## EARLY INTERVENTION

Developmental services, therapy or supports that are provided to a child anytime between birth to entry into first grade.

## INDIVIDUALIZED EDUCATION PLAN OR PROGRAM (IEP)

A plan or program developed to ensure that a child with an identified disability who is attending an elementary or secondary educational institution receives specialized instruction and related services. Typically developed or revised annually with periodic progress reporting. Established by federal law and administered by individual states and school districts.

## IFSP (INDIVIDUALIZED FAMILY SERVICE PLAN)

A written plan developed by an early intervention team to focus on the services that a family needs to help them enhance the development of their child and record the family's desired and achieved outcomes for themselves and their child through age three. An Individual Education Plan (IEP) focuses on educational needs of the child from three to twenty-one.

## LARGE OR GROSS MOTOR SKILLS
Development of large muscle movements that are responsible for running, jumping, crawling, rolling over, and throwing.

## MASKING OR CAMOUFLAGING
The practice of learning and performing certain behaviors and suppressing others in order to be more like neurotypical people. Masking may be subconscious or intentional. Similar to playing a role on stage, this may take the form of someone stimming less obviously, making direct eye contact, and allowing others into their personal space. Another example might be laughing when others laugh without understanding what was funny. Although masking can be a tool someone uses to keep themselves safe in an environment, it often requires a lot of energy to keep up that façade—especially for long periods of time. Sometimes known as "passing" or "passing for NT/Neurotypical."

## MEDICAID AND MEDICARE
Government and employment funded health care programs for persons who cannot afford health insurance or qualify for the program because they are sixty-five or older or disabled.

## MELTDOWN
An intense response to sensory overload or overwhelming circumstances, such as anxiety or distress related to conforming to neurotypical expectations. Meltdowns are characterized by a loss of ability to communicate or control behavior. The function of a meltdown is to release pain and pressure. Often extended periods of calming activity or a change in environment is required to recover ability to communicate and self-control. Efforts to calm a person having a meltdown by touching them or follow directions can make the meltdown worse. Meltdowns are sometimes confused with tantrums, which have a goal of obtaining something from others. Tantrums are typically short and end when the tantrumming person gets what they want. Suppressed meltdowns can manifest as severe migraines or nausea.

## NEURODIVERGENT OR ATYPICAL
A person who thinks differently from what the majority (referred to as neurotypical) expect. Groups of people whose brains are *different* from the typical in how they think/process information, feel, learn, perceive, express thoughts, and/or behave, adding a new dimension to our human culture.

## NEURODIVERSE
A group of people whose brain differences affect how their brain works. Includes autism, Attention Deficit Disorder and Hyperactive Disorder (ADD and ADHD), Down syndrome, and other natural variations on the neurotypical. When embraced and affirmed, people who are neurodivergent bring a new perspective to problem-solving and group decision-making and contribute creative options that might not otherwise be considered.

## NEUROTYPICAL OR TYPICAL
Not displaying, or characterized by autistic, or other neurologically atypical patterns of thought or behavior. Neurotypical individuals sometimes assume that their experience of the world is either the only one or the only correct one, behaving toward or speaking about the atypical in ways that may exhibit explicit or implicit bias.

## OCCUPATIONAL THERAPIST
A specially trained health care professional who uses a scientific basis to promote a person's ability to fulfill their daily routines and roles.

## PHYSICAL THERAPIST
A specially trained health care professional who evaluates and treats human body disorders or illnesses related to a person's bones and muscles; neurological system; heart and lung system; or skin to improve and/or restore functionality.

## PORTFOLIO
A set of creative work or demonstrations of knowledge/skills collected by someone to display their skills to a potential employer. The portfolio may include pictures or examples of work/skills that are carried in a digital or physical website/location, Instagram account, folder, or case.

## POWER OF ATTORNEY OR GUARDIANSHIP
Legal documents defined by laws in your state that give full or limited powers to designated responsible adults to make decisions for, or act on behalf of, persons with disabilities in one or more dimensions of their lives. This could include finances, healthcare, housing, disability services, and activities of daily living.

## SECTION 504 PLAN
Federal requirement that school districts provide a *free appropriate public education* to students in their jurisdictions who have a physical or mental impairment that substantially limits one or more major life activities.

## SENSORY PROCESSING
The mental and/or physical response (or lack of response) of a person to sensory stimuli such as sound, touch, taste, or smell.

## SHUTDOWN
An overwhelmed autistic person's response to their distress from overload. The person gets quiet and less responsive as they block out extra stimuli.

## SMALL OR FINE MOTOR SKILLS
Coordination of your small muscles (like those in your hands, wrists, and fingers) with your eyes. Fine motor skills enable functions such as writing, grasping small objects, and fastening clothing.

## SPECIAL EDUCATION
Specially designed instruction, at no cost to the parents, to meet the unique needs of a child with disabilities including instruction conducted in the classroom, in the home, in hospitals, institutions, and other settings.

## SPEECH THERAPIST
A specially trained health care professional who assesses, diagnoses, and treats speech disorders and communication problems.


## SPOON THEORY
A self-pacing strategy that emphasizes the need for chronic pain patients to work to, or allocate to, a certain quota of activity in daily living. Can be applied to the sensory impacts of ASD and its management. https://www.webmd.com/multiple-sclerosis/features/spoon-theory


## STIM OR STIMMING
Repetitive self-stimulating behavior that have the function of relieving overwhelming sensory stimulation. Examples of stims include sounds, hand flapping, body rocking, spinning, repeated words, or manipulation of objects. Most people stim in subtle ways such as tapping a pencil, biting nails, or twirling hair. Autistic stimming is seen as atypical and more intense or unrestrained.


## SUPPLEMENTAL SECURITY INCOME (SSI) AND SOCIAL SECURITY DISABILITY INSURANCE (SSDI)
Federal Social Security Administration programs for persons with disabilities. Qualification for these two programs that pay monthly benefits to individuals with qualifying disabilities depends on age, work history of adult family members, and income. Research and get help in deciding what benefits are available and best for you and your family at different points in your life. Children and adults are served by both programs. A person may only participate in one, not both.

# INTERVIEW AND RESOURCE CREDITS

1. Trent Pflug

2. Dr. Annette Estes, PhD, Psychologist, Director, University of Washington Autism Center and Center on Human Development and Disability, Seattle, Washington, USA

3. Dr. Sara Woods, PhD, Psychologist, University of Washington Autism Center, Tacoma, Washington, USA

4. Claudia Peterson, RN

5. Sharon Loudon, Autism Education Coordinator, Educational Service District 105, Yakima, Washington, USA

6. Dr. Diane Liebe MD, Developmental and Behavioral Pediatrician and Clinic Medical Director, Children's Village, Yakima, Washington, USA

7. Alyssa Zepp, Occupational Therapist, Children's Village, Yakima, Washington, USA

8. Betty McKinney, special needs educator

9. Dr. Robert Devney, MD, Psychiatrist and Pediatrician, Bothell Psychological Associates, Bothell, Washington, USA

10. Danielle Wood, Parent to Parent, Children's Village, Yakima, Washington, USA

11. Jill Frazier and family

12. Katie Abrams, Director, Washington State University ROAR Program, College of Education, Pullman, Washington, USA

13. Robin Talley, M.Ed., Director of Training and School Services, UW Autism Center, Seattle, Washington, USA

14. Tracie Hoppis, Manager of Family Support Services, Children's Village, Yakima Washington, USA

15. Debi, John and Kim Pflug

16. Connor Desy

17. Carla Thomas, special needs educator

18. Freefall and family

19. Neuroclastic.com (Authors and contributors especially Autistic Science Person)

20. Summer Elliot, caregiver, Independent Living Group Homes

21. Authors of *Older Autistic Adults in Their Own Words: The Lost Generation*, Wilma Wake, Eric Endlich and Robert Lagos

22. Rand Gillen

# REFERENCES ALPHABETICALLY

1. American Psychiatric Association. (2013). *Diagnostic and statistical manual of mental disorders* (DSM 5th ed.). https://doi.org/10.1176/appi.books.9780890425596

2. Arky, B. *Why many autistic girls are overlooked*, Child Mind Institute. https://childmind.org/article/autistic-girls-overlooked-undiagnosed-autism/

3. "Ask an Autistic." YouTube series on autism topics presented by autistic adults. https://www.youtube.com/playlist?list=PLAoYMFsyj_k1ApNj_QUkNgKC1R5F9bVHs

4. "As We See It," Amazon Prime Video, 2022.

5. Attwood, S. (2008). *Making Sense of Sex*. Jessica Kingsley Publishing.

6. *Autcraft* version of *Minecraft* video game. https://www.autcraft.com/.

7. Autism Book list. *Not an Autism Mom*. https://notanautismmom.com/2020/07/20/autism-books/

8. Autism Internet Modules for parents and professionals, free. https://autisminternetmodules.org/

9. Autism Pastor website and publications. Created by an African American pastor on the spectrum.

10. Autistic Hoya – autistic adult self-discovery. https://www.autistichoya.com/

11. Autistic Typing's resources: https://www.facebook.com/AutisticTyping/posts/455214035079000 Links to social media related to people of color who are autistic.

12. Baker, J. (2012). *No More Meltdowns*. Future Horizons.

13. Bal, V.H., Wilkinson, E., & Fok, M. (2021). Cognitive profiles of children with autism spectrum disorder with parent-reported extraordinary talents and personal strengths. *Autism*, 26(1), 62–74. https://doi.org/10.1177/13623613211020618

14. Blazhenkova, O., & Kozhevnikov, M. (2009). The new object-spatial-verbal cognitive style model: theory and measurement. *Applied Cognitive Psychology*. Includes a style questionnaire: "Object-Spatial Imagery and Verbal Questionnaire (OSIVQ).

15. Blazhenkova, O., & Kozhevnikov, M. (2010). Trade-off in object versus spatial visualization abilities: restriction in the development of visual processing resources. *Psychonomic Bulletin & Review*.

16. Bolis, B., Wenderoth, B., & Schilbach, L. (2017). Beyond Autism: Introducing the Dialectical Misattunement Hypothesis and a Bayesian Account of Intersubjectivity, *Psychopathology*.

17. Bulluss, E., & Sesterka, A. (n.d.). Reframing professional language around autism in practice. *Psychology Today*. https://www.psychologytoday.com/us/blog/insights-about-autism/202006/reframing-professional-language-around-autism-in-practice

18. *Center for Disease Control (CDC) Developmental Milestones* resources. https://www.cdc.gov/ncbddd/actearly/milestones/index.html

19. Clarke, J.I., & Dawson, C. (1989). *Growing up again.* Hazelden.

20. Clifton Strengths test. Gallup Inc. (2018). Neurotypical-based and costs money. 34 strengths reported in terms used in neurotypical world. Can use to communicate your personal strengths to an employer.

21. Cook, H. (2021). *The Autistic 10-step plan to making friends.* https://themighty.com/topic/autism-spectrum-disorder/how-to-make-friends-autism

22. Cope & Remington, The strengths and abilities of autistic people in the workplace, March 2022. *Autism in Adulthood.*

23. Crompton, C.J., Hallett, S., Ropar, D., Flynn, E., & Fletcher-Watson, S. (2020). 'I never realized everybody felt as happy as I do when I am around autistic people': A thematic analysis of autistic adults' relationships with autistic and neurotypical friends and family. *Autism*, 24(6), 1438–1448. https://doi.org/10.1177/1362361320908976

24. Crompton, C.J., Ropar, D., Evans-Williams, C.V., Flynn, E.G., & Fletcher-Watson, S. (2020). Autistic peer-to-peer information transfer is highly effective. *Autism*, 24(7), 1704–1712. https://doi.org/10.1177/1362361320919286

25. Devenish, B.D., Mantilla, A., Bowe, S.J., Grundy, E.A.C., & Rinehart, N.J. (2022). Can common strengths be identified in autistic young people? A systematic review and meta-analysis. *Research in Autism Spectrum Disorders*, 98, 102025. https://doi.org/10.1016/j.rasd.2022.102025.

26. Deweerdt, S. (2020). Repetitive behaviors and 'stimming' behavior in autism explained. spectrumnews.org

27. Diversity in Social Intelligence Research. http://dart.ed.ac.uk/research/nd-iq/

28. Donvan, J., and Zucker, C. (2016). *In a different key: The story of autism.* Broadway Books.

29. Encyclopedia Britannica Human Physiology.https://www.britannica.com/science/information-theory/Physiology.

30. Harrington, L. (2021). *Finding the right autism services for your child*, University of Washington Autism Center.

31. Franco, M. (2022). *Platonic: How the science of attachment can help you make and keep friends.* Putnam.

32. Winter-Messiers, M.A. (2021). From tarantulas to toilet brushes: Understanding the special interest areas of children and youth with Asperger syndrome, *Remedial and Special Education*.

33. Garnett, M. and Attwood, T. (2021). *Autism working: A seven-stage plan to thriving at work.* Jessica Kingsley Publishing.

34. Gillespie-Lynch, K., Kapp, S.K., Shane-Simpson, C., Smith, D.S., & Hutman, T. (2014). Intersections between the autism spectrum and the internet: Perceived benefits and preferred functions of computer-mediated communication. *Intellectual and Developmental Disabilities*, 52(6), 456–469. https://doi.org/10.1352/1934-9556-52.6.456

35. Google Operations Research. (2019). https://academy.nobl.io/google-high-performing-teams/

36. Grandin, T. (2008). *Developing talents.* Future Horizons.

37. Grandin, T., & Moore, D. (2021). *Navigating autism: Nine mindsets for helping kids on the spectrum.* W.W. Norton & Company.

38. Grandin, T., & Panek, R. (2014). *The autistic brain: Helping different kinds of minds succeed.*

39. Haciomeroglu, E. (2016). Object-spatial visualization and verbal cognitive styles and their relation to cognitive abilities and mathematical performance.

40. Harmuth, E., Silletta, E., Bailey, A., Adams, T., Beck, C., & Barbic, S. P. (2018). Barriers and facilitators to employment for adults with autism: A scoping review. *Annals of International Occupational Therapy*, 1(1), 31–40. https://doi.org/10.3928/24761222-20180212-01

41. Hertz, M. (2020). Edutopia: Tools for creating digital student portfolios. https://www.edutopia.org/article/tools-creating-digital-student-portfolios

42. Honeybourne, V. (2019). *The neurodiverse workplace*, Jessica Kingsley.

43. How to respectfully talk about disability. https://www.npr.org/2022/08/08/1115682836/how-to-talk-about-disability-sensitively-and-avoid-ableist-tropes;

44. Hudson, C., Hall, H., and Harkness, K. (2019). Prevalence of depressive disorders in individuals with Autism Spectrum Disorder (ASD): A meta-analysis, *Journal of Abnormal Child Psychology*.

45. Hull, L., Petrides, K.V., Allison, C., Smith, P., Baron-Cohen, S., Lai, M.C., & Mandy, W. (2017). "Putting on my best normal": Social camouflaging in adults with autism spectrum conditions. *Journal of Autism and Developmental Disorders, 47,* 2519–2534.

46. Hunt, J. (2021). *Life Coaching for Adults on the Autism Spectrum: Discovering Your Potential.* ASD Life Coaches LLC.

47. Kapp, S., Gillespie-Lynch, K., Sherman, L., & Hutman, T. (2013). Deficit, difference, or both? Autism and neurodiversity, *Developmental Psychology.*

48. Kapp, S.K., Steward, R., Crane, L., Elliott, D., Elphick, C., Pellicano, E., & Russell, G. (2019). 'People should be allowed to do what they like': Autistic adults' views and experiences of stimming. *Autism, 23(7),* 1782–1792.

49. Kirchner, J., Ruch, W., & Dziobek, I. (2016). Brief report: Character strengths in adults with autism spectrum disorder without intellectual impairment. *Journal of Autism and Developmental Disorders, 46(10),* 3330–3337. doi:10.1007/s10803-016-2865-7.

50. Kluth, P., & Schwarz, P. (2010). *Just give him the whale! 20 Ways to use fascinations, areas of expertise, and strengths to support students with autism.* Baltimore: Paul H. Brookes.

51. Kontra, C., Goldin-Meadow, S., & Bellock, S. (2012). Embodied learning across the life span, *Topics in Cognitive Science.* https://onlinelibrary.wiley.com/doi/full/10.1111/j.1756-8765.2012.01221.x

52. Kranowitz, C.S. (2022). *Out of sync child* and *the out of sync child grows up.* TarcherPerigee.

53. Laber-Warren, E. (2021). The benefits of focused interests in autism. https://www.spectrumnews.org/features/deep-dive/the-benefits-of-special-interests-in-autism/

54. Lee, G. K., & Carter, E. W. (2012). Preparing transition-age students with high-functioning autism spectrum disorders for meaningful work. *Psychology in the Schools, 49(10),* 988–1000. https://doi.org/10.1002/pits.21651. Identifies seven promising elements of successful high school transition services.

55. LifeCourse Nexus. An online resource for life planning of the University of Missouri. https://www.lifecoursetools.com/

56. Life skills assessment tools: Assessment of Functional Living Skills (AFLS) including independent living https://functionallivingskills.com/ (Partington and Mueller) and Essentials for Living https://essentialforliving.com/about-us/ (McGreevy).

57. Lion, S. (2020). *Finding your autistic superpower: A practical handbook for woman and girls on the autism spectrum.*

58. Marsh, W. *Recognizing autism in women and girls.*

59. Mottron, L. Research and publications on strengths-based education for and strengths of persons affected with ASD. Research papers related to strengths in executive function, visual function, auditory function, and other areas.

60. Mottron, L., Bouvet, L., Bonnel, A., Samson, F., Burack, J. A., Dawson, M., et al. (2013). Veridical mapping in the development of exceptional autistic abilities. *Neuroscience and Biobehavioral Reviews*, 37(2), 209–228. doi:10.1016/j.neubiorev.2012.11.016

61. National Autistic Society UK. (2020). Making friends – a guide for autistic adults. https://www.autism.org.uk/advice-and-guidance/topics/family-life-and-relationships/making-friends/autistic-adults

62. National Centers for Disease Control and Prevention (CDC). Autism resources on screening, diagnosis and development. https://www.cdc.gov/ncbddd/autism/facts.html

63. Nerenberg, J. (2020). *Divergent minds: Thriving in a world that was not designed for you.* HarperCollins.

64. Neuroclastic.com. A website for and by adults on the autism spectrum.

65. Nuewer, R. (2021). Finding strengths in autism. *Spectrum Research News*. https://www.spectrumnews.org/features/deep-dive/finding-strengths-in-autism/

66. Nuewer, R. (2020) Growing old with autism. *Spectrum Research News*. https://www.spectrumnews.org/features/deep-dive/growing-old-with-autism/

67. Open Doors for Multicultural Families. https://www.multiculturalfamilies.org/

68. "Outschool." An online learning platform pursuing education through exploring focused interests. https://outschool.com/about#abl8z6mwqe

69. PAVE. https://wapave.org/

70. Project Based Learning (PBL) for Students with Autism. (2019). https://speedypaper.com/essays/project-based-learning-pbl-for-students-with-autism.

71. Puberty and autism: An unexplored transition. (2021). https://www.spectrumnews.org/features/deep-dive/puberty-and-autism-an-unexplored-transition/

72. Reframing Autism, Celebrating and nurturing Autistic identity. https://reframingautism.org.au/

73. Remington, A., & Fairnie, J. (2017). A sound advantage: Increased auditory capacity in autism. *Cognition*, 166, 459–465. doi:10.1016/j.cognition.2017.04.002

74. Reifman, C., and Arnett, J. (2007). Emerging adulthood: Theory, assessment and application, *Journal of Youth Development*.

75. Russell, G., Kapp, S. K., Elliott, D., Elphick, C., Gwernan-Jones, R., & Owens, C. (2019). Mapping the autistic advantage from the accounts of adults diagnosed with autism: A qualitative study. *Autism in Adulthood*.

76. Schlooz, W. A., & Hulstijn, W. (2014). Boys with autism spectrum disorders show superior performance on the adult Embedded Figures Test. *Research in Autism Spectrum Disorders*.

77. Shah, P., Catmur, C. & Bird, G. Emotional decision-making in autism spectrum disorder: The roles of interoception and alexithymia. *Molecular Autism*.

78. Sigman, M., & Capps, L. (1997). *Children with autism: A developmental perspective*. Harvard University Press.

79. Snell-Rood, C., Ruble, L., Kleinert, H., McGrew, J.H., Adams, M., Rodgers, A., Odom, J., Wong, W.W., Yu, Y. (2020). Stakeholder perspectives on transition planning, implementation and outcomes for students with autism spectrum disorder. *Autism*.

80. Soulieres, I., Zeffiro, T.A., Girard, M.L., & Mottron, L. (2011). Enhanced mental image mapping in autism. *Neuropsychologia*.

81. Spectrum Research News Special Report. (2021). Autistic strengths and special interests by various authors. https://www.spectrumnews.org/features/legacy-special-reports/special-report-autistic-strengths-and-special-interests/

82. Stevenson, J.L., & Gernsbacher, M.A. (2013). Abstract spatial reasoning as an autistic strength. *PloS One*, Special note: Names non-verbal test of intelligence in abstract Distinquishes sub tests in various areas – 27 AT adults outperformed on all.

83. Robson. (2019). Ten Positive Traits that Some People with Autism Have, CBC. https://www.cbc.ca/parents/learning/view/i-want-to-share-10-positive-traits-that-people-with-autism-have

84. Teti, M., Cheak-Zamora, N., Lolli, B., & Maurer-Batjer, A. (2016). Reframing autism: Young adults with autism share their strengths through photo-stories. *Journal of Pediatric Nursing*. Special note topics 1) focused interests that cultivated positive emotions and coping strategies; 2) skills and activities that evoked pride; and 3) reframing ASD as special versus a disadvantage. Used photo voice or participatory art method for expressing strengths https://www.youtube.com/watch?v=QVoWxGOIqyQ photovoice YouTube

85. *The Black Autist*. https://blackautist.wordpress.com. Blog created by an African American adult man on the spectrum.

86. *The Spectrum*. (2013–2019). Magazine written by and for people on the autism spectrum, quarterly. https://www.autism.org.uk/advice-and-guidance/the-spectrum

87. *The Sniffer*, Netflix series, 2013–2019.

88. Thomas, V. (2007). *Winnie and Wilbur: Winnie the Witch*. HarperCollins.

89. University of Washington Autism Center, Seattle, Washington. https://depts.washington.edu/uwautism/training/uwactraining/ Training for parents and professionals.

90. Nichols, J. 12 *Educational Apps To Create Digital Portfolios*. https://www.teachthought.com/technology/create-digital-portfolios/

91. Umucu, E., Lee, B., Genova, H.M., Chopik, W. J., Sung, C., Yasuoka, M., & Niemiec, R.M. (2022). Character strengths across disabilities: An international exploratory study and implications for positive psychiatry and psychology. *Frontiers in Psychiatry*, 13. https://doi.org/10.3389/fpsyt.2022.863977

92. *Videos:*

    a. *Ask an Autistic* vlog (series of videos on YouTube) on autism topics presented by autistic adults. https://www.youtube.com/playlist?list=PLAoYMFsyj_k1ApNj_QUkNgKC1R5F9bVHs

    b. Autistic Identity in the African Diaspora by Timotheus T.J. Gordon: https://www.youtube.com/watch?v=CcaOfXo7mHA

    c. McCabe, Jessica. "Try Different." https://www.youtube.com/watch?v=evathYHc1Fg&t=228s

    d. "Meet Julia" *Sesame Street* Video on Autism: https://www.youtube.com/watch?v=dKCdV20zLMs&t=196s

    e. Nine positive traits (that you may not already know) https://www.youtube.com/watch?v=OvZVOlVnQW0

    f. University of Washington *Autism Stories*: https://depts.washington.edu/uwautism/communityengagement/autismstories/

    g. Watson, Crompton, et al. Diversity in Social Intelligence Research University of Edinburgh, U.K. 2021. Video of findings: https://www.youtube.com/watch?v=dEvg4tbiEhU. Research: http://dart.ed.ac.uk/research/nd-iq/

93. Visual cues list, Autistic Awareness Center. https://autismawarenesscentre.com/visual-supports-best-way-use/

94. Voss, A. (2011). *Understanding your child's sensory signals*, CreateSpace Independent Publishing Platform.

95. Wake, W., Endlich, W., & Lagos, R. (2021). *Older autistic adults in their own words: The lost generation.* Future Horizons.

96. Walker, S.C., Williams, K., & Moore, D.J. (2020). Superior identification of component odors in a mixture is linked to autistic traits in children and adults. *Chemical Senses.*

97. Warren, N., Eatchel, B., Kirby, A.V., Diener, M., Wright, C., & D'Astous, V. (2020). Parent-identified strengths of autistic youth. *Autism: The International Journal of Research and Practice.*

98. Webinars of special note University of Washington Autism Center (free):

    a. *Could I Be Autistic?* (for teenagers and adults)

    b. *Introduction to Neurodiversity and Autistic Culture for Parents of Young Children* (for parents)

    c. *Neurodiversity-Affirming Autism Assessment Across the Lifespan: A Strengths-Based Approach* prerecorded; for providers, 3 APA CEs, 3 BBS California CEUs, 3 IL CEUs and 3 WA clock hours) Dr. Sara Woods, PhD Psychology.

99. Wehman, P., Smith, M. & Schall, C. (2009). *Autism and the transition to adulthood: Success beyond the classroom.* Paul Brookes Publishing.

100. Weishaar, P.M. (2010). Twelve ways to incorporate strengths-based planning into the IEP process. *The Clearing House: A Journal of Educational Strategies, Issues and Ideas*, 83(6), 207–210. https://doi.org/10.1080/00098650903505381

101. Wilkinson, E., Vo, L., London, Z., Wilson, S., & Hal, V.H. (2022). Parent-Reported Strengths and Positive Qualities of Adolescents and Adults with Autism Spectrum Disorder and/or Intellectual Disability. *Journal of Autism and Developmental Disorders*, https://doi.org/10.1007/s10803-021-05405-x Online ahead of print.

102. Winner, M.G., and Crooke, P. (2020). *You are a social detective! explaining social thinking to kids*, 2nd ed. Social Thinking. Plus additional social skills resources for youth and young adults from the same publisher.

103. Wood, R. (2019) Autism, intense interests and support in school: From wasted efforts to shared understandings. *Educational Review.*

104. Wylie, P., Lawson, W., & Beardon, L. (2016). *The nine degrees of autism: A developmental model.* Routledge.

105. Yasuda, Y., Hashimoto, R., Nakae, A., Kang, H., Ohi, K., Yamamori, H., et al. (2016). Sensory cognitive abnormalities of pain in autism spectrum disorder: A case-control study. *Annals of General Psychiatry.*

106. Yeager, K.H., & Deardorff, M.E. (2021). Strengths-based transition planning: A positive approach for students with learning disabilities. *Intervention in School and Clinic,* 58(1), 3–8. https://doi.org/10.1177/10534512211047594

107. Zhuang, F., and Liao, Y. (2017). Want more? learn less: Motivation affects adolescents learning from negative feedback, *Developmental Psychology.*

108. Yi, B. (2020). *Individual psychological factors and thinking styles and their role in camouflaging behaviours and trajectories in autistic and non-autistic people: A quantitative and qualitative study.* ProQuest Dissertations Publishing.

109. Zeliadt, N. (2018). Revealing autism's hidden strengths. *Spectrum Research News.* spectrumnews.org. Examples of persons with autism who speak few or no words and discussion of testing.

# REFERENCES BY TOPIC

## 1. Autistic adults

a. Nuwer, R (2020). Growing Old with Autism. Spectrum Research News. https://www.spectrumnews.org/features/deep-dive/growing-old-with-autism/

b. Wake, W., Endlich, W., & Lagos, R. (2021) *Older autistic adults in their own words: The lost generation.* Future Horizons.

## 2. Autism affirming testing and language

a. Bulluss, E., & Sesterka, A. (n.d.). Reframing professional language around autism in practice. *Psychology Today.* https://www.psychologytoday.com/us/blog/insights-about-autism/202006/reframing-professional-language-around-autism-in-practice

b. Diversity in Social Intelligence Research. http://dart.ed.ac.uk/research/nd-iq/

c. How to respectfully talk about disability. https://www.npr.org/2022/08/08/1115682836/how-to-talk-about-disability-sensitively-and-avoid-ableist-tropes.;

d. Kapp, S., Gillespie-Lynch, K., Sherman, L., & Hutman, T. (2013) Deficit, difference, or both? Autism and neurodiversity, *Developmental Psychology.*

e. Neuroclastic.com, a website for and by adults on the autism spectrum.

f. Neurodiversity-Affirming Autism Assessment Across the Lifespan: A Strengths-Based Approach prerecorded; for providers, 3 APA CEs, 3 BBS California CEUs, 3 IL CEUs and 3 WA clock hours) Dr. Sara Woods, PhD Psychology. (Pre-recorded Webinar for providers) University of Washington Autism Center

g. Teti, M., Cheak-Zamora, N., Lolli, B., & Maurer-Batjer, A. (2016). Reframing autism: Young adults with autism share their strengths through photo-stories. *Journal of Pediatric Nursing.* Special note topics 1) focused interests that cultivated positive emotions and coping strategies; 2) skills and activities that evoked pride; and 3) reframing ASD as special versus a disadvantage. Used photo, voice or participatory art method for expressing strengths https://www.youtube.com/watch?v=QVoWxGOIqyQ photovoice YouTube

h. Yeager, K. H., & Deardorff, M. E. (2021). Strengths-based transition planning: A positive approach for students with learning disabilities. *Intervention in School and Clinic*, 58(1), 3–8. https://doi.org/10.1177/10534512211047594

a. American Psychiatric Association. (2013). *Diagnostic and statistical manual of mental disorders* (DSM 5th ed.). https://doi.org/10.1176/appi.books.9780890425596

b. *Could I Be Autistic?* (Free Pre-recorded Webinar for teenagers and adults) University of Washington Autism Center

c. Donvan, J., and Zucker, C. (2016). *In a different key: The story of autism*. Broadway Books.

d. Grandin, T., & Panek, R. (2014). *The autistic brain: Helping different kinds of minds succeed.* Mariner Books.

e. Hull, L., Petrides, K. V., Allison, C., Smith, P., Baron-Cohen, S., Lai, M. C., & Mandy, W. (2017). "Putting on my best normal": Social camouflaging in adults with autism spectrum conditions. *Journal of Autism and Developmental Disorders, 47,* 2519–2534.

f. "Meet Julia" *Sesame Street* Video on Autism: https://www.youtube.com/watch?v=dKCdV20zLMs&t=196s

g. National Centers for Disease Control and Prevention (CDC) Autism resources on screening, diagnosis and development. https://www.cdc.gov/ncbddd/autism/facts.html

h. Neurodiversity-Affirming Autism Assessment Across the Lifespan: A Strengths-Based Approach prerecorded webinar; for providers, 3 APA CEs, 3 BBS California CEUs, 3 IL CEUs and 3 WA clock hours) Dr. Sara Woods, PhD Psychology.

i. Soulieres, I., Zeffiro, T.A., Girard, M.L., & Mottron, L. (2011) Enhanced mental image mapping in autism. *Neuropsychologia.*

j. Stevenson, J. L., & Gernsbacher, M. A. (2013). Abstract spatial reasoning as an autistic strength. *PloS One,* Special note: Names non-verbal test of intelligence in abstract Distinguishes sub tests in various areas – 27 AT adults outperformed on all.

k. Wake, W., Endlich, W., & Lagos, R. (2021). *Older autistic adults in their own words: The lost generation.* Future Horizons.

l. Wylie, P., Lawson, W., & Beardon, L. (2016). *The nine degrees of autism: A developmental model.* Routledge.

m. Zeliadt, N. (2018). Revealing autism's hidden strengths. *Spectrum Research News.* spectrumnews.org. Examples of persons with autism who speak few or no words and discussion of testing.

## 4. Calming and stamina

a. Baker, J. (2012). *No More Meltdowns.* Future Horizons

b. Deweerdt, S. (2020). Repetitive behaviors and 'stimming' behavior in autism explained. spectrumnews.org

c. Kapp, S. K., Steward, R., Crane, L., Elliott, D., Elphick, C., Pellicano, E., & Russell, G. (2019). 'People should be allowed to do what they like': Autistic adults' views and experiences of stimming. *Autism*, 23(7), 1782–1792.

d. Kluth, P., & Schwarz, P. (2010). *Just give him the whale! 20 Ways to use fascinations, areas of expertise, and strengths to support students with autism.* Baltimore: Paul H. Brookes.

e. Meng-Chuan Lai, Peter Szatmari, Journal article *Resilience in Autism: Research and Practice Prospects,* 2019;

f. Teti, M., Cheak-Zamora, N., Lolli, B., & Maurer-Batjer, A. (2016). Reframing autism: Young adults with autism share their strengths through photo-stories. *Journal of Pediatric Nursing.* Special note topics 1) focused interests that cultivated positive emotions and coping strategies; 2) skills and activities that evoked pride; and 3) reframing ASD as special versus a disadvantage. Used photo, voice or participatory art method for expressing strengths https://www.youtube.com/watch?v=QVoWxGOIqyQ photovoice YouTube

g. Voss, Angie (2011), Understanding Your Child's Sensory Signals, CreateSpace Independent Publishing Platform.

## 5. Developmental stages

a. Center for Disease Control (CDC) Developmental Milestones resources. https://www.cdc.gov/ncbddd/actearly/milestones/index.html

b. Clarke, J. I., & Dawson, C. (1989). *Growing up again.* Hazelden.

c. Early Start Denver Model therapists for infant/toddler intervention. https://www.esdm.co/;

d. Hull, L., Petrides, K. V., Allison, C., Smith, P., Baron-Cohen, S., Lai, M. C., & Mandy, W. (2017). "Putting on my best normal": Social camouflaging in adults with autism spectrum conditions. *Journal of Autism and Developmental Disorders*, 47, 2519–2534.

e. Kontra C, Goldin-Meadow S. & Bellock, S. (2012). Embodied learning across the life span, *Topics in cognitive science.* https://onlinelibrary.wiley.com/doi/full/10.1111/j.1756-8765.2012.01221.x

f. *Neurodiversity-Affirming Autism Assessment Across the Lifespan: A Strengths-Based Approach* prerecorded; for providers, 3 APA CEs, 3 BBS California CEUs, 3 IL CEUs and 3 WA clock hours) Dr. Sara Woods, PhD Psychology. (Pre-recorded Webinar for providers) University of Washington Autism Center

g. Sigman, M., & Capps, L. (1997). *Children with autism: A developmental perspective.* Harvard University Press.

h. Wake, W., Endlich, W., & Lagos, R. (2021). *Older autistic adults in their own words: The lost generation.* Future Horizons.

i. Wylie, P., Lawson, W., & Beardon, L. (2016). *The nine degrees of autism: A developmental model.* Routledge.

## 6. *Education (IEP) and transition planning*

a. Grandin, Temple (2008) *Developing Talents.* Future Horizons.

b. Life skills assessment tools are Assessment of Functional Living Skills (AFLS) including independent living https://functionallivingskills.com (Partington and Mueller) and Essentials for Living https://essentialforliving.com/about-us/ (McGreevy).

c. List of 22 College and University level transitions programs funded by the US Department of Education (https://www2.ed.gov/programs/tpsid/awards.html)

d. PAVE. https://wapave.org/

e. Reifman, Colwell and Arnett, Emerging Adulthood: Theory, assessment and application, *Journal of Youth Development,* 2007.

f. Skills and interests survey coupled with a person-centered plan that includes a "circles of support" element. Example: https://portal.ct.gov/-/media/DDS/FactSheets/ifs_pcp.pdf.

g. Snell-Rood, C., Ruble, L., Kleinert, H., McGrew, J.H., Adams, M., Rodgers, A., Odom, J., Wong, W> W., Yu, Y. (2020). Stakeholder perspectives on transition planning, implementation and outcomes for students with autism spectrum disorder. *Autism.*

h. Teti, M., Cheak-Zamora, N., Lolli, B., & Maurer-Batjer, A. (2016). Reframing autism: Young adults with autism share their strengths through photo-stories. *Journal of Pediatric Nursing.* Special note topics 1) focused interests that cultivated positive emotions and coping strategies; 2) skills and activities that evoked pride; and 3) reframing ASD as special versus a disadvantage. Used photo voice or participatory art method for expressing strengths https://www.youtube.com/watch?v=QVoWxGOIqyQ photovoice YouTube

i.    Nichols, J. *12 Educational Apps To Create Digital Portfolios*. https://www.teachthought.com/technology/create-digital-portfolios/

j.    Warren, N., Eatchel, B., Kirby, A. V., Diener, M., Wright, C., & D'Astous, V. (2020). Parent-identified strengths of autistic youth. Autism : The International Journal of Research and Practice

k.    Wehman, P., Smith, M. & Schall, C.(2009). *Autism and the transition to adulthood: Success beyond the classroom.* Paul Brookes Publishing.

l.    Weishaar, P. M. (2010). Twelve ways to incorporate strengths-based planning into the IEP process. *The Clearing House: A Journal of Educational Strategies, Issues and Ideas*, 83(6), 207–210. https://doi.org/10.1080/00098650903505381

m.   Wylie, P., Lawson, W., & Beardon, L. (2016). *The nine degrees of autism: A developmental model.* Routledge.

n.    Yeager, K. H., & Deardorff, M. E. (2021). Strengths-based transition planning: A positive approach for students with learning disabilities. *Intervention in School and Clinic*, 58(1), 3–8. https://doi.org/10.1177/10534512211047594

## 7. *Employment*

a.    Clifton Strengths test. Gallup Inc., 2018. (Neurotypical-based and costs money. 34 strengths reported in terms used in neurotypical world. Use this to communicate your personal strengths to an employer).

b.    Cope & Remington, *The strengths and abilities of autistic people in the workplace*, March 2022

c.    Garnett, M. and Attwood, T. (2021). *Autism working: A seven-stage plan to thriving at work.* Jessica Kingsley Publishing.

d.    Google Operations Research. (2019). https://academy.nobl.io/google-high-performing-teams/

e.    Harmuth, E., Silletta, E., Bailey, A., Adams, T., Beck, C., & Barbic, S. P. (2018). Barriers and facilitators to employment for adults with autism: A scoping review. *Annals of International Occupational Therapy*, 1(1), 31–40. https://doi.org/10.3928/24761222-20180212-01

f.    Hertz, M. (2020). Edutopia: Tools for creating digital student portfolios. https://www.edutopia.org/article/tools-creating-digital-student-portfolios

g.    Honeybourne, V. (2019). *The Neurodiverse Workplace*, Jessica Kingsley.

h. Hunt, J. (2021). *Life Coaching for Adults on the Autism Spectrum: Discovering Your Potential.* ASD Life Coaches LLC.

i. Lee, G. K., & Carter, E. W. (2012). Preparing transition-age students with high-functioning autism spectrum disorders for meaningful work. *Psychology in the Schools,* 49(10), 988–1000. https://doi.org/10.1002/pits.21651 Identifies seven promising elements of successful high school transition services.

j. Project Based Learning (PBL) for Students with Autism. (2019, Oct 08). Retrieved from https://speedypaper.com/essays/project-based-learning-pbl-for-students-with-autism.

k. Wehman, P., Smith, M. & Schall, C.(2009). *Autism and the transition to adulthood: Success beyond the classroom.* Paul Brookes Publishing.

## 8. *Focused interests*

a. Kluth, P., & Schwarz, P. (2010). *Just give him the whale! 20 Ways to use fascinations, areas of expertise, and strengths to support students with autism.* Baltimore: Paul H. Brookes.

b. "Outschool," an online learning platform pursuing education through exploring focused interests. https://outschool.com/about#abl8z6mwqe

c. Teti, M., Cheak-Zamora, N., Lolli, B., & Maurer-Batjer, A. (2016). Reframing autism: Young adults with autism share their strengths through photo-stories. *Journal of Pediatric Nursing.* Special note topics 1) focused interests that cultivated positive emotions and coping strategies; 2) skills and activities that evoked pride; and 3) reframing ASD as special versus a disadvantage. Used photo, voice or participatory art method for expressing strengths https://www.youtube.com/watch?v=QVoWxGOIqyQ photovoice YouTube

d. *The Sniffer,* Netflix series 2013 to 2019

e. Winter-Messiers, Mary Ann. From Tarantulas to Toilet Brushes: Understanding the Special Interest Areas of Children and Youth with Asperger Syndrome, *Remedial and Special Education Journal,* 2007.

f. Wood, R. (2019) *Autism, intense interests and support in school: From wasted efforts to shared understandings.* Educational Review.

## 9. *General resources*

a. ARC resources in your state: https://thearc.org/;

b. Autism Book list by Not an Autism Mom https://notanautismmom.com/2020/07/20/autism-books/

c. Autism Internet Modules for parents and professionals free. https://autisminternetmodules.org/

d. *Could I Be Autistic?* (Free Pre-recorded Webinar for teenagers and adults) University of Washington Autism Center

e. *Finding the right autism services for your child* by Dr. Lucas Harrington, PsyD, University of Washington Autism Center, 2021

f. Grandin, T., & Moore, D. (2021). *Navigating autism: Nine mindsets for helping kids on the spectrum.* W.W. Norton & Company.

g. Grandin, T., & Panek, R. (2014). *The autistic brain: Helping different kinds of minds succeed.* Mariner Books.

h. LifeCourse Nexus, an online resource for life planning of the University of Missouri. https://www.lifecoursetools.com/

i. Parent-to-parent support and networking groups in your area at https://www.p2pusa.org/

j. Training for parents and professionals. University of Washington Autism Center, Seattle, Washington https://depts.washington.edu/uwautism/training/uwactraining/

## 10. *Identity, social interaction, and autistic culture*

a. Autistic Identity in the African Diaspora by Timotheus T.J. Gordon: https://www.youtube.com/watch?v=Cca0fXo7mHA(Video)

b. Crompton, C. J., Hallett, S., Ropar, D., Flynn, E., & Fletcher-Watson, S. (2020). 'I never realized everybody felt as happy as I do when I am around autistic people': A thematic analysis of autistic adults' relationships with autistic and neurotypical friends and family. *Autism,* 24(6), 1438–1448. https://doi.org/10.1177/1362361320908976

c. Crompton, C. J., Ropar, D., Evans-Williams, C. V., Flynn, E. G., & Fletcher-Watson, S. (2020). Autistic peer-to-peer information transfer is highly effective. *Autism,* 24(7), 1704–1712. https://doi.org/10.1177/1362361320919286

d. Diversity in Social Intelligence Research. http://dart.ed.ac.uk/research/nd-iq/

e. Gillespie-Lynch, K., Kapp, S. K., Shane-Simpson, C., Smith, D. S., & Hutman, T. (2014). Intersections between the autism spectrum and the internet: Perceived benefits and preferred functions of computer-mediated communication. *Intellectual and Developmental Disabilities,* 52(6), 456–469. https://doi.org/10.1352/1934-9556-52.6.456

f. Grandin, T., & Moore, D. (2021). *Navigating autism: Nine mindsets for helping kids on the spectrum*. W.W. Norton & Company.

g. Hull, L., Petrides, K. V., Allison, C., Smith, P., Baron-Cohen, S., Lai, M. C., & Mandy, W. (2017). "Putting on my best normal": Social camouflaging in adults with autism spectrum conditions. *Journal of Autism and Developmental Disorders*, 47, 2519–2534.

h. Introduction to Neurodiversity and Autistic Culture for Parents of Young Children (for parents) Free webinar University of Washington, Autism Center.

i. "Meet Julia" *Sesame Street* Video on Autism: https://www.youtube.com/watch?v=dKCdV20zLMs&t=196s

j. Neuroclastic.com, a website for and by adults on the autism spectrum.

k. RecRoom social application. https://recroom.com/

l. Reframing Autism, Celebrating and nurturing Autistic identity https://reframingautism.org.au/

m. *The Spectrum magazine* written by and for people on the autism spectrum, quarterly. https://www.autism.org.uk/advice-and-guidance/the-spectrum

n. "Try Different" song by Jessica McCabe https://www.youtube.com/watch?v=evathYHc1Fg&t=228s

o. University of Washington "Autism Stories": https://depts.washington.edu/uwautism/communityengagement/autismstories/

p. Wake, W., Endlich, W., & Lagos, R. (2021). *Older autistic adults in their own words: The lost generation*. Future Horizons.

q. Watson, Crompton, et al. Diversity in Social Intelligence Research University of Edinburgh, U.K. 2021. Video of findings: https://www.youtube.com/watch?v=dEvg4tbiEhU. Research: http://dart.ed.ac.uk/research/nd-iq/

r. Winner, M.G., and Crooke, P. (2020). *You are a social detective! explaining social thinking to kids*, 2nd ed. Social Thinking. Plus additional social skills resources for youth and young adults from the same publisher.

## 11. *Learning and cognitive styles*

a. Blazhenkova, O, & Kozhevnikov, M (2009). The new object-spatial-verbal cognitive style model: theory and measurement. *Applied Cognitive Psychology*. Includes a style questionnaire: "Object-Spatial Imagery and Verbal Questionnaire (OSIVQ).

b.  Blazhenkova, O, & Kozhevnikov, M. (2010) Trade-off in object versus spatial visualization abilities: restriction in the development of visual processing resources. *Psychonomic Bulletin & Review.*

c.  Kontra C, Goldin-Meadow S. & Bellock, S. (2012). Embodied learning across the life span, Topics in cognitive science. https://onlinelibrary.wiley.com/doi/full/10.1111/j.1756-8765.2012.01221.x

d.  Visual cues list, Autistic Awareness Center. https://autismawarenesscentre.com/visual-supports-best-way-use/

e.  Walker, S.C., Williams, K., & Moore, D.J. (2020). Superior identification of component odors in a mixture is linked to autistic traits in children and adults. *Chemical Senses.*

f.  Warren, N., Eatchel, B., Kirby, A.V., Diener, M., Wright, C., & D'Astous, V. (2020). Parent-identified strengths of autistic youth. Autism : *The International Journal of Research and Practice.*

g.  Yi, B. (2020). *Individual Psychological Factors and Thinking Styles and Their Role in Camouflaging Behaviours and Trajectories in Autistic and Non-Autistic People: A Quantitative and Qualitative Study* (dissertation). ProQuest Dissertations Publishing.

h.  Zhuang, Feng and Liao, Want More? Learn Less: Motivation Affects Adolescents Learning from Negative Feedback, January 2017 *Developmental Psychology.*

## 12. *Neurodivergent people of color*

a.  Autistic Identity in the African Diaspora by Timotheus T.J. Gordon: https://www.youtube.com/watch?v=CcaOfXo7mHA

b.  Autism Pastor website and publications. Created by an African American pastor on the spectrum.

c.  Autistic Typing's resources: https://www.facebook.com/AutisticTyping/posts/455214035079000 Links to social media related to people of color who are autistic.

d.  Open Doors for Multicultural Families https://www.multiculturalfamilies.org/

e.  Nerenberg, J. (2020). *Divergent minds: Thriving in a world that was not designed for you.* HarperCollins.

f.  The Black Autist website. https://blackautist.wordpress.com/Blog created by an African American adult man on the spectrum.

## 13. *People on the spectrum who are non-speaking*

a. Stevenson, J. L., & Gernsbacher, M. A. (2013). Abstract spatial reasoning as an autistic strength. *PloS One*, Special note: Names non-verbal test of intelligence in abstract. Distinguishes sub tests in various areas – 27 AT adults outperformed on all.

b. Teti, M., Cheak-Zamora, N., Lolli, B., & Maurer-Batjer, A. (2016). Reframing autism: Young adults with autism share their strengths through photo-stories. *Journal of Pediatric Nursing*. Special note topics 1) focused interests that cultivated positive emotions and coping strategies; 2) skills and activities that evoked pride; and 3) reframing ASD as special versus a disadvantage. Used photo voice or participatory art method for expressing strengths https://www.youtube.com/watch?v=QVoWxGOIqyQ photovoice YouTube

c. Zeliadt, N. (2018). Revealing autism's hidden strengths. *Spectrum Research News*. spectrumnews.org. Examples of persons with autism who speak few or no words and discussion of testing.

## 14. *Portfolios*

a. Hertz, M. (2020). Edutopia: Tools for creating digital student portfolios. https://www.edutopia.org/article/tools-creating-digital-student-portfolios

b. Project Based Learning (PBL) for Students with Autism. (2019, Oct 08). Retrieved from https://speedypaper.com/essays/project-based-learning-pbl-for-students-with-autism.

c. Teti, M., Cheak-Zamora, N., Lolli, B., & Maurer-Batjer, A. (2016). Reframing autism: Young adults with autism share their strengths through photo-stories. *Journal of Pediatric Nursing*. Special note topics 1) focused interests that cultivated positive emotions and coping strategies; 2) skills and activities that evoked pride; and 3) reframing ASD as special versus a disadvantage. Used photo, voice or participatory art method for expressing strengths https://www.youtube.com/watch?v=QVoWxGOIqyQ photovoice YouTube

d. Nichols, J. 12 Educational Apps To Create Digital Portfolios. https://www.teachthought.com/technology/create-digital-portfolios/

## 15. *Self-awareness*

a. "As We See It," Amazon Prime Video, 2022.

b. *Autism Pastor* website and publications. Created by an African American pastor on the spectrum.

c. "Autism Stories." University of Washington. https://depts.washington.edu/uwautism/communityengagement/autismstories/

d.  Autistic Hoya (blog) – autistic adult self-discovery. https://www.autistichoya.com/

e.  Autistic Typing. https://www.facebook.com/AutisticTyping/posts/455214035079000 Links to social media related to people of color who are autistic.

f.  *Could I Be Autistic?* University of Washington Autism Center. Free pre-recorded webinar for teenagers and adults.

g.  Hudson, C., Hall, H., and Harkness, K. (2019). Prevalence of depressive disorders in individuals with autism spectrum disorder (ASD): a meta-analysis, *Journal of Abnormal Child Psychology.*

h.  Hull, L., Petrides, K. V., Allison, C., Smith, P., Baron-Cohen, S., Lai, M. C., & Mandy, W. (2017). "Putting on my best normal": Social camouflaging in adults with autism spectrum conditions. *Journal of Autism and Developmental Disorders, 47,* 2519–2534.

i.  Neuroclastic.com. A website for and by adults on the autism spectrum.

j.  Remington, A., & Fairnie, J. (2017). A sound advantage: Increased auditory capacity in autism. *Cognition,* 166, 459–465. doi:10.1016/j.cognition.2017.04.002

k.  Russell, G., Kapp, S. K., Elliott, D., Elphick, C., Gwernan-Jones, R., & Owens, C. (2019). Mapping the autistic advantage from the accounts of adults diagnosed with autism: A qualitative study. *Autism in Adulthood.*

l.  Teti, M., Cheak-Zamora, N., Lolli, B., & Maurer-Batjer, A. (2016). Reframing autism: Young adults with autism share their strengths through photo-stories. *Journal of Pediatric Nursing.* Special note topics 1) focused interests that cultivated positive emotions and coping strategies; 2) skills and activities that evoked pride; and 3) reframing ASD as special versus a disadvantage. Used photo, voice or participatory art method for expressing strengths https://www.youtube.com/watch?v=QVoWxGOlqyQ photovoice YouTube

m.  McCabe, J. "Try Different." https://www.youtube.com/watch?v=evathYHc1Fg&t=228s

n.  Wake, W., Endlich, W., & Lagos, R. (2021). *Older autistic adults in their own words: The lost generation.* Future Horizons.

o.  Wylie, P., Lawson, W., & Beardon, L. (2016). *The nine degrees of autism: A developmental model.* Routledge.

## 16. *Sex*

a. "As We See It," Amazon Prime Video, 2022.

b. Attwood, S. (2008). *Making sense of sex.* Jessica Kingsley Publishing.

c. Puberty and autism: An unexplored transition. (2021). https://www.spectrumnews.org/features/deep-dive/puberty-and-autism-an-unexplored-transition/

## 17. *Social skill building*

a. *Autcraft* version of *Minecraft* video game (https://www.autcraft.com/.

b. Cook, H. (2021). The Autistic 10-step plan to making friends. https://themighty.com/topic/autism-spectrum-disorder/how-to-make-friends-autism

c. Franco, M. (2022). *Platonic: How the science of attachment can help you make and keep friends.* Putnam.

d. Hunt, J. (2021). *Life Coaching for Adults on the Autism Spectrum: Discovering Your Potential.*

e. National Autistic Society UK. (2020). Making friends – a guide for autistic adults. https://www.autism.org.uk/advice-and-guidance/topics/family-life-and-relationships/making-friends/autistic-adults

f. Watson, Crompton, et al. Diversity in Social Intelligence Research University of Edinburgh, U.K. 2021. Video of findings: https://www.youtube.com/watch?v=dEvg4tbiEhU. Research: http://dart.ed.ac.uk/research/nd-iq/

## 18. *Strengths and abilities*

a. Bal, V. H., Wilkinson, E., & Fok, M. (2021). Cognitive profiles of children with autism spectrum disorder with parent-reported extraordinary talents and personal strengths. *Autism*, 26(1), 62–74. https://doi.org/10.1177/13623613211020618

b. Devenish, B. D., Mantilla, A., Bowe, S. J., Grundy, E. A. C., & Rinehart, N. J. (2022). Can common strengths be identified in autistic young people? A systematic review and meta-analysis. *Research in Autism Spectrum Disorders*, 98, 102025. https://doi.org/10.1016/j.rasd.2022.102025.

c. Diversity in Social Intelligence Research. http://dart.ed.ac.uk/research/nd-iq/

d. Kirchner, J., Ruch, W., & Dziobek, I. (2016). Brief report: Character strengths in adults with autism spectrum disorder without intellectual impairment. *Journal of Autism and Developmental Disorders*, 46(10), 3330–3337. doi:10.1007/s10803-016-2865-7

e. Mottron, L. Research and publications on strengths-based education for and strengths of persons affected with ASD. Research papers related to strengths in executive function, visual function, auditory function, and other areas.

f. Mottron, L., Bouvet, L., Bonnel, A., Samson, F., Burack, J. A., Dawson, M., et al. (2013). Veridical mapping in the development of exceptional autistic abilities. *Neuroscience and Biobehavioral Reviews*, 37(2), 209–228. doi:10.1016/j.neubiorev.2012.11.016

g. Neurodiversity-Affirming Autism Assessment Across the Lifespan: A Strengths-Based Approach prerecorded; for providers, 3 APA CEs, 3 BBS California CEUs, 3 IL CEUs and 3 WA clock hours) Dr. Sara Woods, PhD Psychology. (Pre-recorded Webinar for providers) University of Washington Autism Center

h. Nine positive traits (that you may not already know) https://www.youtube.com/watch?v=OvZVOlVnQW0

i. Nuewer, R. (2021). Finding strengths in autism. Spectrum Research News. https://www.spectrumnews.org/features/deep-dive/finding-strengths-in-autism/

j. Remington, A., & Fairnie, J. (2017). A sound advantage: Increased auditory capacity in autism. *Cognition*, 166, 459–465. doi:10.1016/j.cognition.2017.04.002

k. Robson. (2019). Ten Positive Traits that Some People with Autism Have, CBC. https://www.cbc.ca/parents/learning/view/i-want-to-share-10-positive-traits-that-people-with-autism-have

l. Russell, G., Kapp, S. K., Elliott, D., Elphick, C., Gwernan-Jones, R., & Owens, C. (2019). Mapping the autistic advantage from the accounts of adults diagnosed with autism: A qualitative study. *Autism in Adulthood.*

m. Schlooz, W. A., & Hulstijn, W. (2014). Boys with autism spectrum disorders show superior performance on the adultEnbedded Figures Test. *Research in Autism Spectrum Disorders.*

n. Shah, P., Catmur, C. & Bird, G. Emotional decision-making in autism spectrum disorder: The roles of interoception and alexithymia. *Molecular Autism.*

o. Spectrum Research News Special Report: Autistic strengths and special interests by various authors, 2021. https://www.spectrumnews.org/features/legacy-special-reports/special-report-autistic-strengths-and-special-interests/

p. Stevenson, J. L., & Gernsbacher, M. A. (2013). Abstract spatial reasoning as an autistic strength. *PloS One*, Special note: Names non-verbal test of intelligence in abstract Distinquishes sub tests in various areas – 27 AT adults outperformed on all.

q.   Teti, M., Cheak-Zamora, N., Lolli, B., & Maurer-Batjer, A. (2016). Reframing autism: Young adults with autism share their strengths through photo-stories. *Journal of Pediatric Nursing.* Special note topics 1) focused interests that cultivated positive emotions and coping strategies; 2) skills and activities that evoked pride; and 3) reframing ASD as special versus a disadvantage. Used photo, voice or participatory art method for expressing strengths https://www.youtube.com/watch?v=QVoWxGOIqyQ photovoice YouTube

r.   *The Sniffer,* Netflix series 2013 to 2019

s.   "Try Different" song by Jessica McCabe https://www.youtube.com/watch?v=evathYHc1Fg&t=228s

t.   Umucu, E., Lee, B., Genova, H. M., Chopik, W. J., Sung, C., Yasuoka, M., & Niemiec, R. M. (2022). Character strengths across disabilities: An international exploratory study and implications for positive psychiatry and psychology. *Frontiers in Psychiatry,* 13. https://doi.org/10.3389/fpsyt.2022.863977

u.   University of Washington "Autism Stories": https://depts.washington.edu/uwautism/communityengagement/autismstories/

v.   Watson, Crompton, et al. Diversity in Social Intelligence Research University of Edinburgh, U.K. 2021. Video of findings: https://www.youtube.com/watch?v=dEvg4tbiEhU. Research: http://dart.ed.ac.uk/research/nd-iq/

w.   Wilkinson, E., Vo, L., London, Z., Wilson, S., & Hal, V.H. (2022). Parent-Reported Strengths and Positive Qualities of Adolescents and Adults with Autism Spectrum Disorder and/or Intellectual Disability. *Journal of Autism and Developmental Disorders,* https://doi.org/10.1007/s10803-021-05405-x . Online ahead of print.

x.   Yasuda, Y., Hashimoto, R., Nakae, A., Kang, H., Ohi, K., Yamamori, H., et al. (2016). Sensory cognitive abnormalities of pain in autism spectrum disorder: A case-control study. *Annals of General Psychiatry.*

y.   Zeliadt, N. (2018). Revealing autism's hidden strengths. *Spectrum Research News.* spectrumnews.org. Examples of persons with autism who speak few or no words and discussion of testing.

## 19.  *Women and girls on the spectrum*

a.   Arky, Beth, Why many Autistic Girls are Overlooked, Child Mind Institute. https://childmind.org/article/autistic-girls-overlooked-undiagnosed-autism/

b.   Hull, L., Petrides, K. V., Allison, C., Smith, P., Baron-Cohen, S., Lai, M. C., & Mandy, W. (2017). "Putting on my best normal": Social camouflaging in adults with autism spectrum conditions. *Journal of Autism and Developmental Disorders,* 47, 2519–2534.

c.  Lion, S. (2020). *Finding your autistic superpower: A practical handbook for woman and girls on the autism spectrum.* Self Published.

d.  Marsh, W. *Recognizing Autism in Women and Girls.*

e.  Nerenberg, J. (2020). *Divergent minds: Thriving in a world that was not designed for you.* HarperCollins.

f.  Thomas, V (2007). *Winnie and Wilbur: Winnie the Witch.* HarperCollins.

g.  Wake, W., Endlich, W., & Lagos, R. (2021). *Older autistic adults in their own words: The lost generation.* Future Horizons.

# ANNE'S BIO

Retiring after 40 years of service in local government, I also taught public sector management and research at Central Washington University in my hometown of Ellensburg, Washington and at the University of Washington, Seattle, Evans Graduate School of Public Policy. I have three adult children, two of whom are neurodivergent. I was proactive in my children's education and care. I participated in parent support groups and as a member of the local county Developmental Disability Board. As a single head of household with an autistic adult child living at home, I share the experience of the majority of families in the country with household members on the spectrum. I hold an MBA in Management and Finance from Seattle University and a BA with an emphasis in community planning from The Evergreen State College in Washington State. I currently enjoy a range of creative pursuits and being active in my community.

Printed in the USA
CPSIA information can be obtained
at www.ICGtesting.com
JSHW060608220124
55737JS00004B/8